Interdisciplinary Teaching

Alvin M. White, *Editor*

NEW DIRECTIONS FOR TEACHING AND LEARNING

KENNETH E. EBLE and JOHN F. NOONAN, *Editors-in-Chief*

Number 8, December 1981

Paperback sourcebooks in
The Jossey-Bass Higher Education Series

Jossey-Bass Inc., Publishers
San Francisco • Washington • London

Interdisciplinary Teaching
Number 8, December 1981
    Alvin M. White, *Editor*

New Directions for Teaching and Learning Series
Kenneth E. Eble and John F. Noonan, *Editors-in-Chief*

New Directions for Teaching and Learning is published quarterly
by Jossey-Bass Inc., Publishers. Subscriptions, single-issue
orders, change of address notices, undelivered copies, and other
correspondence should be sent to *New Directions* Subscriptions,
Jossey-Bass Inc., Publishers, 433 California Street, San Francisco,
California 94104.

Editorial correspondence should be sent to the Editors-in-Chief,
Kenneth E. Eble or John F. Noonan, Center for Improving
Teaching Effectiveness, Virginia Commonwealth University,
Richmond, Virginia 23284.

Library of Congress Catalogue Card Number LC 80-84304
International Standard Serial Number ISSN 0271-0633
International Standard Book Number ISBN 87589-869-6

Cover art by Willi Baum
Manufactured in the United States of America

Ordering Information

The paperback sourcebooks listed below are published quarterly and can be ordered either by subscription or as single copies.

Subscriptions cost $30.00 per year for institutions, agencies, and libraries. Individuals can subscribe at the special rate of $18.00 per year *if payment is by personal check.* (Note that the full rate of $30.00 applies if payment is by institutional check, even if the subscription is designated for an individual.) Standing orders are accepted.

Single copies are available at $6.95 when payment accompanies order, and *all single-copy orders under $25.00 must include payment.* (California, Washington, D.C., New Jersey, and New York residents please include appropriate sales tax.) For billed orders, cost per copy is $6.95 plus postage and handling. (Prices subject to change without notice.)

To ensure correct and prompt delivery, all orders must give either the *name of an individual* or an *official purchase order number.* Please submit your order as follows:

Subscriptions: specify series and subscription year.
Single Copies: specify sourcebook code and issue number (such as TL8).

Mail orders for United States and Possessions, Latin America, Canada, Japan, Australia, and New Zealand to:
Jossey-Bass Inc., Publishers
433 California Street
San Francisco, California 94104

Mail orders for all other parts of the world to:
Jossey-Bass Limited
28 Banner Street
London EC1Y 8QE

New Directions for Teaching and Learning Series
Kenneth E. Eble and John F. Noonan, *Editors-in-Chief*

Contents

Editor's Notes

". . . The specialist 'knows' very well his own corner of the universe; he is radically ignorant of all the rest. . . . Previously men could be divided simply into the learned and the ignorant. . . . But your specialist cannot be brought in under either of these two categories. He is not learned, for he is formally ignorant of all that does not enter into his specialty; but neither is he ignorant, because he is 'a scientist', and 'knows' very well his own portion of the universe. We shall have to say that he is a learned ignoramus. . . . Anyone who wishes can observe the stupidity of thought, judgment, and action shown today in politics, art, religion, and the general problems of life and the world by the 'men of science' and of course, behind them, the doctors, engineers, financiers, teachers, and so on. The state of 'not listening' . . . reaches its height precisely in these partially qualified men."

—Jose Ortega y Gasset, *The Revolt of the Masses*

Interdisciplinarity is sometimes a slogan, sometimes a goal, often a topic of controversy, and always a concept that is defined in a personal way. What is its relevance in a sourcebook series on teaching and learning? Is it an antidote for the two cultures described by C. P. Snow? Is it a response to Ortega y Gasset's description of the specialist? Is it a boost to liberal learning?

Interdisciplinarity may be all of the above. Our concern with teaching and learning leads us to note that faculty as well as students suffer from the narrow organization of education. A narrow focus on specialized content actually diminishes comprehension of the content itself. There are aspects of a subject which are unnoticed or invisible until we view them from a distance or from the perspective of another subject.

Significant knowledge is naturally interdisciplinary. If we seek understanding, then we cannot restrict the scope of inquiry. If we want to encourage the discovery of hidden connections or similarities by others or ourselves, if we want to create an environment for serendipity, then our teaching and learning should reflect these objectives.

Is the creation of an environment for serendipity a reasonable goal? Is there a way of encouraging students to expect the unexpected? Can such an environment be created in a single classroom independent of the institution? I think that the answer to these questions is yes, but the tasks are neither obvious nor easy. Teachers and students should learn that connections are not discovered as often as they are invented.

Each author in this sourcebook was asked to contribute a chapter on interdisciplinary teaching and learning. The variety of responses is an indication that connections are abundant and essential. Each author is associated with a single discipline in a college or university. Some discuss interdisciplinarity, some describe classroom experiences, and others mention neither explicitly. All are tied together by the search for understanding; all invent connections that can serve as examples and models. Our own encounters with each chapter are opportunities or challenges to find connections in mode or content with our own teaching and learning. The teacher's contribution is not so much information as it is a point of view or approach.

Getting Beyond the Disciplines

Geoffrey Vickers's wide-ranging chapter touches on many of the themes found in subsequent chapters. He writes of two modes of understanding: causal and contextual, and the relation between teaching and learning. He considers the scope and needs of interdisciplinarity from the point of view of the teacher and of the learner, and observes how slight an acquaintance with any subject is sufficient for the nonspecialist. His hope is that teachers should be "absorbed by the excitement of passing on what they know and engaging interest, especially in what they do not know but long to know and believe to be knowable." He conjectures that "less structured and less specialized teaching might result in quicker learning even of the specialties."

Ralph Ross's chapter deals with the folly of specialization and compartmentalization at the elementary as well as the graduate level. "Experience alone is no teacher; it can condition response but it cannot impart principles. That is reserved for reflection as it plays on experience." The "sciences give us a fulcrum to move the world. But if we don't use the fulcrum with care, we dislodge ourselves. What is the meaning and value of the events we can create or destroy? That is what the humanities study."

These chapters by Vickers and Ross can each stand alone, but together they create a synergistic effect. Each is an illustration for the other, as our perception of one colored square is dynamically influenced by an adjoining colored square.

The third chapter is by Kenneth Boulding, one of the founders of the Society for General Systems Research. He observes that interest in general systems came from several sources. One has the "feeling among practitioners in a number of different fields that any investigation of a practical problem of some system in the real world had to transcend the conventional disciplinary lines because the real world was not really divided according to the usual disciplines. . . . The inability of the real world to be compartmentalized means that any kind of problem-solving activity requires an interest in the general system that underlies the problem and cannot be confined to any one discipline." He observes that "systems themselves change in a systematic way. . . .

We see this very clearly in the evolutionary process where evolution itself evolves, that is, the process itself changes, as one process realizes its potential."

Education can be thought of as part of the societal evolution that produces human artifacts. "Human knowledge and valuations," Boulding writes, "can also be seen as species in the language ecosystem and subject to the same kind of evolutionary processes." The slow growth of the general systems enterprises within higher education is an example of the difficulties that most interdisciplinary efforts face. Yet, like other such movements, general systems evolved because, in Boulding's words, "the real world was not really divided according to the usual disciplines." And, despite the fact that "disciplines are the strongest unit in both the academic and professional communities, and are suspicious of anything which seems to erode their boundaries," Boulding's chapter and the others in this volume testify to the "hankering for a larger view, a broader perspective than can be found in single departments or disciplines."

How are a snow crystal, an insulin molecule, a Bach chorale, and a painting by Mondrian related? David Layzer's chapter sketches out a possible answer, beginning with a consideration of geometric, physical, and biological order. He finds that whereas the biologist relates the order of an insulin molecule to function, the question of functional order has no meaning to a physicist. The function or "fitness" of a protein depends upon the biological context, just as the meaning or fitness of a word depends on the context. The impression that every word and phrase in a poem is uniquely determined by its context arises in the same way as the unity of a biological organism and represents the same kind of order.

Interdisciplinarity helps us to understand why a question may be crucial in one context and meaningless in another, and how insight and ideas in seemingly unrelated disciplines can illuminate such a fundamental question as the nature of order in the universe. Ralph Ross, in his earlier chapter, stresses the necessary connection between the sciences and the humanities. The sciences, he writes, "explain how things occur and the humanities explore the possible meanings and values of the things that occur . . . the humanities offer a complement to the power that science gives us, for they help us choose the ends for which we use power, the human goals we must never forget."

This concern with ends and human goals is at the center of C. West Churchman's chapter about the value assumptions that underlie individual subject matters. Both teachers and students have an obligation to identify these value assumptions, both within and across disciplines. For, Churchman believes, "it is as important to understand the interconnectedness of aspects of a system as it is to understand the aspects themselves." Making connections is a creative event of teaching and learning. In many cases, the connection did not exist until it was created by someone. Even a trivial connection can serve as an example and can encourage additional examples. Each day's homework assignment can include searching for connections with concepts or items in other courses—past, present, or future. As a help for that assignment, the class session can end with a review of the concepts discussed that day in order to know what concepts are at one of the terminals of the connections. Such a review has value for other reasons. The fabric of ideas that is woven in Churchman's chapter is rich in suggestiveness about teaching and learning and about relating professors and students.

Examples of Interdisciplinary Teaching

Two examples have been chosen to illustrate interdisciplinary teaching and learning. One is on the large scale of Evergreen College, one of the most consequential outcomes of the innovative and interdisciplinary spirit of the sixties. As Richard Jones points out, the college "has no departments, requirements, majors, courses, or grades. Instead, groups of students and small teams of faculty contract to work together full-time (for a semester, a year, or two years) to study a theme, solve a problem, or complete a project of interdisciplinary scope."

An unexpected consequence of the interdisciplinary program at Evergreen is described in Jones's chapter about the "dream reflection-creative writing seminar." Personal though it was in idea and inception, it was taken up and adapted to the individual teaching styles of a dozen colleagues. The course also forced its creator to expand his own insights by exposure to the works of Polanyi, Piaget, Langer, Marcuse, and others. The author's comments that "consideration of *what* is learned are secondary to considerations of *how* to learn" repeats a theme of other chapters in this volume. The occurrence of common themes follows naturally from the intentions of the authors to consider questions without disciplinary constraints. It is the author's belief that he might not have discovered and written about the dream poet if he had followed conventional paths. While describing the emergence of his own insights, Jones shares with the reader a description of an alternative community and the effects of its inner dynamics.

The second example is a detailed description of an interdisciplinary course recently developed at Harvard by Arthur Loeb. Cross-disciplinary courses can be found in most colleges and universities across the country. Many, like the course Loeb describes, are grounded in the humanities and arts where history provides a framework while verbal texts and visual arts provide a substance that helps define a culture at a given time and place. Loeb's course deals with political, art, music, dance, and literary history in medieval Burgundy. The period, 1350–1530, was a transitional period from the Middle Ages to the Renaissance and was important to the formation of modern European states. The flourishing of the arts amidst the political complexities of the Burgundian domains provided a rich context for examining and trying to recreate the life of that time. The contributions and interdependence of the many departments that participated are evident. The excitement and involvement of students, faculty, and others who followed a path of learning that combined personal experience with academic study can be shared by the reader.

Interdisciplinary Scholarship

Interdisciplinary teaching and learning may always be at some cross-purpose with disciplinary commitments because most scholarship is done within the disciplines and, increasingly, within subspecializations of the disciplines. Nevertheless, scholars past and present have done distinguished work that crosses disciplinary boundaries. Owen Gingerich's chapter about the astrological allusions in the poems of Chaucer, Skelton, and Donne is informed by the expertise of the author, an astrophysicist and professor of astronomy. In turn, the chapter acknowledges its debt to the work of Chaucerian scholars — English professors who turned to scientific colleagues and knowledge to assist them in understanding Chaucer's world and work. Gingerich's descriptions of the consulted sources of information show the interdependence of many disciplines for an understanding of literary works. The author's narrative also demonstrates the possibility of scholarly collaboration across disciplinary boundaries. The poems indicate that at the time they were written, scientific knowledge was of interest and was available to a more general population than now. Interdisciplinarity became an issue only after specialization became the norm.

The quotation from John Donne used by Gingerich in referring to Galileo and Kepler is also cited by Barbara Mowat in the second of these interdisciplinary chapters. The influence of Kepler's *De stella nova* and Galileo's *Siderieus nuncius* is mentioned by both authors. Each shows how the seventeenth century was a time of new discoveries and philosophies that were shared with or at least commented upon by poets.

The overlap of the two chapters is strongly suggestive of the role of interdisciplinary content on the process of teaching and learning. Our teaching must be informed by ideas and concerns beyond our nominal discipline — not for the sake of interdisciplinarity, but in order to understand and appreciate that single discipline. And, since we are teaching students, it behooves us to understand the psychology of students and of learning.

Can we re-create in our classrooms the excitement that accompanied the discoveries that are our subject matter? Michael Polanyi, in *Personal Knowledge* (1964, p. 172), contrasts the classroom teaching with the subject being taught: "A transition takes place . . . from a heuristic act to the routine teaching and learning of its results. . . . The impulse which in the original heuristic act was a violent irreversible self-conversion of the investigator" and an almost equally "tempestuous process of converting others . . . will assume finally a form in which all dynamic quality is lost."

Perhaps the loss of the dynamic quality is due to the loss of the connections that our subject has with others, and the loss of understanding of the allusions used. The chapters in this volume can serve as models of interdisciplinary connectedness. The variety of subjects is an opportunity and a challenge to find those connections for our own subjects and to involve our students in heuristic understanding.

What Makes Teaching and Learning Interdisciplinary?

In the first of the final group of chapters, Carl Hertel looks at energy and architecture to discuss the manner in which contexts affect the way we are shaped by and reflect back upon the surrounding environment. Urbanization, he argues, affects our sense of esthetics: "Where the technological assumes primary importance, poetics . . . are sacrificed to technique." Could our classrooms be included in the description, "The impersonality of the technically inspired environment has destroyed the sense of place characterizing earlier architecture"?

Teaching and learning are interdisciplinary in ways that are beyond the connections that can be made among disciplines. The environment of the classroom has an effect on learning. The arrangement of chairs in rows or a circle is influential on learning. A nourishing breakfast has been found to significantly affect how well primary grade students learn.

Teaching is affected by the same forces that influence other human activities. The points of view that correct answers are more important than understanding, or that the syllabus should be restricted to questions and answers that can be graded by computer are expressions of the primacy of the technological in education. The aims and opportunities of education are topics that transcend disciplines, but impinge on all disciplines.

What makes teaching and learning interdisciplinary? Is it the proximity of two or more disciplines in a course? Or is it connections made with other disciplines? Interdisciplinary teaching depends not so much on the existence of several disciplines as it depends on the existence of a point of view toward the subject matter and toward knowledge in general. It is not so much the content as it is the context and the mode of teaching. In cases where the courses are taught by a team from different departments, it is possible that the separate strands will remain unconnected; that each discipline will retain its isolation. Team taught courses are not automatically interdisciplinary. It is, however, possible for courses taught by one teacher on single subjects to be interdisciplinary if connections with other subjects are sought or an effort is made to overcome the isolation of the subject.

A comparison with other disciplines can sometimes enhance one's understanding of both disciplines. An example of connections that could be made within a single course is a study of time. In Newtonian mechanics, time can proceed forward or backward. In biology and geology, time is one directional. The comparison would make explicit the role of time in each discipline. It could, for example, also illuminate the current controversy about the applicability to economics of mathematical models which come from Newtonian mechanics.

Another example of connections within a single course would be the search for the important concepts or ideas of the subject. Is there a concept as influential in the subject as evolution is in biology? How have the concepts themselves evolved? Have the fundamental questions or philosophical underpinnings changed? What are some unanswered questions of the subject, and why are they important, are considerations which would enrich the course in an interdisciplinary direction.

Even if we consider a single narrow discipline, experts will declare that their subject is more than just facts or techniques to be memorized. But that "something more" is difficult to make part of the course or to make explicit. Examples of approaches that might reveal insights into that something more exist in each subject. Mathematics students might be asked to invent their own problems or to create a word problem corresponding to a symbolic problem or vice versa. Music students might consider the effects of the time of composition on the performing technique. Biology students might seek evidence of adaptation in systems or species. Another activity that might expose the essence of the subject beyond the facts and techniques is to consider the, perhaps unexpected, influences that triggered important breakthroughs in a discipline. For example, Einstein attributes decisive influence on his own thinking to the philosophical writings of David Hume and Ernst Mach despite his differences with them. A knowledge of the diverse sources which contribute to fundamental concepts in a discipline might give the student an appreciation of that "something more" which permeates a subject.

In the spirit of interdisciplinary teaching and learning, we can borrow a concept from linguistics in evaluating students. Linguists use the term productivity in a special way. They consider the extraordinary output of new sentences by people out of their stock of words and syntax. It is this that makes human language such a revealing mirror and so powerful a tool of the mind and spirit. The same test can be used to encourage understanding in many subjects at every level. What can the student do with what she knows to make a "new sentence"? Traditionally, what is tested is not the ability to make a new sentence but the ability to repeat a learned one, at best somewhat rephrased.

Miroslav Holub, who has been called the most important poet working in Europe today, is chief research immunologist at the Institute for Clinical and Experimental Medicine in Prague. Lewis Thomas, author of *Lives of a Cell*, comments about Holub in the foreword to his book of poems, *Sagittal Section* (Holub, 1980): "In real life (scientists and poets) are engaged in the same kind of game. What they are looking for and sometimes, when they are good at their jobs, finding are the points of connections between things in the world which seem to most people unconnected. They live out their lives in puzzlement and wonder, and when they are sufficiently skilled and lucky they achieve that most satisfying of all sensations available to the human mind: surprise. To be able to use one's own brain to generate one's own astonishment at the connectedness of things in the world is not an ordinary accomplishment, not many poets succeed in this, nor many scientists, but this is what they are up to, trying for."

Holub's two poems exhibit humor and the recognition of connectedness. The interdisciplinary spirit is evident in the poems as it is in the other chapters of this volume. It is the nature of interdisciplinarity as a spirit of teaching and learning that a precise formula is impossible. If we set out to discover, we cannot know what we will discover. But we can prepare ourselves and our students to be receptive to the new, to be skeptical about the old, to be personally involved in the search for knowledge, and to respond to any knowledge as we respond to art, by personally experiencing it.

I have included a description of a seminar on teaching and learning that I conducted at M.I.T. in 1976 as the next chapter. Process and environment both were important in achieving the multidisciplinary goals of this seminar. The substance was nominally not in my field (mathematics) and the twelve students were from biology, computer science, artificial intelligence, electrical engineering, environmental studies, linguistics, mathematics, physics, and visual arts. The questions that we considered in the seminar are common to all disciplines and, therefore, are studied by very few: How do people obtain knowledge? What are the limits of certainty? What is the relation between general and scientific knowledge? What is the role of beauty, simplicity, or intuition in creative discovery?

What we learned and how we learned it were quite unexpected. Love and trust were as central to the success of the seminar as they are commonly missing as items in a syllabus for a course or the table of contents of a text. My reflection on the specific experience has a wide applicability, I think, to much teaching and learning: "A narrow focus on the body of knowledge of a discipline is counterproductive. A narrow focus actually diminishes comprehension of specialized content. Specialized knowledge cannot be obtained in isolation from its supporting surroundings, or in isolation from the personal feelings of the learners and teachers."

The volume concludes with a note about ideas, further sources of information, and other activities about interdisciplinary programs.

The chapters which follow are examples of interdisciplinarity. You will find connections within and among them. The new physics tells us that an observer cannot observe without altering what she observes. Observer and observed are interrelated in a real and fundamental sense. The reader and what is read are also interrelated because the reader's perception and response give meaning to what is written.

Alvin M. White
Editor

References

Holub, M. *Sagittal Section*. (S. Friebert and D. Habora, Trans.) The FIELD Translation Series, Vol. 3. Oberlin, Ohio: Oberlin College, 1980.

Ortega y Gasset, J. *The Revolt of the Masses*. New York: Norton, 1957.

Polanyi, M. *Personal Knowledge*. New York: Harper & Row, 1964.

Alvin M. White is professor of mathematics at Harvey Mudd College of the Claremont Consortium. From 1977 to 1981 he was the initiator-director of the project New Interdisicplinary, Holistic Approaches to Teaching and Learning that was supported by the Fund for the Improvement of Postsecondary Education.

Education is more than the process by which teachers at all levels reproduce their kind. Must its contribution to professsional expertise and to human excellence be so patchy and so strangely packaged?

Three Needs, Two Buckets, One Well

Geoffrey Vickers

Teachers at all levels are expected to meet three needs that, however, are not confined to three mutually exclusive classes of students. Traditionally, they must, first and foremost, reproduce their own kind—teachers, dons, and specialists in whatever branch of skill and knowledge provides their own standing and support. Secondly, they must provide whatever academic quotient is needed for a host of professionals. Thirdly, they are still expected by a few, largely outside their own ranks, to transmit from the vast human heritage that selection of skill and knowledge that is most needed by those of their contemporaries who wish to be competent and responsible members of the societies into which they were born.

In universities, the distinction between the first and second need has always been marked by the distinction between academic disciplines and professional schools. These have different tests of relevance. The former asks, What must I do in order to know; the second, What must I know in order to do? The professions dine à la carte at the tables of the disciplines, seeking what they want where they can find it and looking for it themselves if no discipline seems interested. Viruses might never have been discovered by biologists if some viruses had not also been pathogens and therefore moved doctors to seek what were called "filter-passing bacteria." The relations between professional schools and academic disciplines have never been easy and they grow no easier.

A. White (Ed.). *New Directions for Teaching and Learning: Interdisciplinary Teaching*, no. 8.
San Francisco: Jossey-Bass, December 1981

The criteria of relevance used by the professions are normally wider than those used by the disciplines; but they differ much from one profession to another—engineering, medicine, law, education, architecture, planning, policy making, and so on. The criteria widen along the spectrum almost enough to include the needs of ordinary man. (A category that includes professionals and even academics.)

The third class is the most numerous, whether or not its members are also subsumed in the first or second class. The needs of the third class are easily stated. They need the best answer to be found in their age to the questions What am I? Where am I? How did we get here? and What does it require of me? It is fashionable to suppose that the third question and still more the fourth no longer concern us, but this assumption, I believe, is gravely wrong. For the place we find ourselves is partly of our own making and partly the making of our ancestors, and it is only one frame in a rapidly running time sequence. We can understand the present moment only with a lively sense of time and some vague assumptions about the contribution made by human initiative in the process of which we are a part. The answer to the fourth question can best be found by discovering how that (always personal) question has been answered in the past by the most admired members of our own culture and that of other peoples—not the least of history's contribution to our education.

I have never seen what seemed to me effective interdisciplinary work—still less transdisciplinary work—done by an intermixing of disciplines. I have seen it done in professional schools; but some of the professional schools are in danger of becoming bastard and second-class disciplines, looked down on by the "pure" disciplines for their lack of purity and by the professions they serve for their lack of relevance. The professions must share some of the blame for this, because some of them have tended to offload their ancient responsibility for transmitting their skills to their novices and, at the same time, have blamed the universities for failing to transmit a kind of skill that universities never purported to have. Academic medicine has partly solved the problem by swallowing whole that part of the real world in which its most dramatic skills are practiced, namely, the hospitals. It is a solution not open to other professions and it has its costs, notably its relative inattention to the far larger volume of sickness that at any one time is to be found in the world of the well.

The needs of the third class are sometimes dismissed on the grounds that no one today can be more than a specialist. In my view, this is absurd. Of course, it is true that everyone is bound to know more about some things than others and to know nothing at all about other things that conceivably may be important to them. It remains true that we can give a far more comprehensive, even though a much less confident, answer than ever before to the four questions that, as I have suggested, sum up the aspiration for a general education. If we have to teach uncertainties, we can do so. We have always lived with uncertainty, and skill in understanding and accepting it is one of the most basic skills of human life. It does not follow, of course, that teachers and dons are best qualified to teach it. But they should, at least, learn not to mask it.

The fact that there is little transdisciplinary or even interdisciplinary teaching does not mean, of course, that there is no transdisciplinary or inter-disciplinary learning. Specialty cooks can produce menus from which varied and even balanced meals can be chosen. Only let them remember that, between them, their job is to produce the makings of a good meal for the guests, not a host of specialized cooks. It is an ancient educational problem to decide how far educators should spread the table, how far they should press their particular wares, and how far they should insist that, like it or not, some particular skill or knowledge must be absorbed. These are not alternatives; all are needed. Ours is not a world in which, for example, we can leave the unwill-ing reader illiterate. Equally, no condition is more basic for teaching than that the teacher's passion for the subject should be apparent to the learner, whether the learner learns to share it or not. Yet there is also need and room for the learner's choice—for only the student can do the learning.

Nor need the subjects necessarily be packaged for the supposed conve-nience of the learner. I once took, simultaneously, two short courses, one in European history from 1789 to 1870 and the other in French romantic litera-ture. They were not linked in any way and they were taught by different lec-turers but no one needed to tell me that they would be complementary. Per-haps they should have been linked, at least in one way, for it is rash, to say the least, to study the literature of an age without knowing its historical and cul-tural background. I know a teacher who suffered acute anguish from being forced to let children read their first Shakespeare play without a moment's introduction to the history and culture of the age in which it was written.

The example leads one to ask whether problems of interdisciplinary teaching and learning are the same in the humanities, the logical sciences, the experimental and observational sciences, and those unclassified fields where the subject matter is historical. Some of these have earned the prestigious name of sciences—geology, evolutionary biology, and even ecology. Some have not, notably human history, including the history of science and the his-tory of culture (of which the history of science is a part). Human history seems to me to be the most preeminently necessary field of study for general educa-tion and, though it can be divided both into periods and into fields of special concern, it seems to me that these divisions are less likely to divide practition-ers than the divisions of the natural sciences.

But are the problems the same? The question raises another question of vital importance and universal neglect—the nature and extent of background knowledge needed to support any specialty and the source from which this background is derived.

Naturally, specialists are unwilling to admit how slight an acquain-tance with any subject, especially their own, is sufficient for nearly all non-specialist purposes. The law, for example, is a massive and complicated subject. Yet every citizen is supposed to "know the law" and it very seldom happens that anyone gets into trouble from ignorance or misunderstanding of the law, even though, so far as I know, it receives little or no attention at any stage of education except for lawyers. Of course many people go to lawyers for advice on matters that involve points of law, but they usually know when to go and they usually understand what a lawyer tells them. I, who was trained in the law, but had no education in natural science, have an awareness of many fields of natural science that is sufficient to place me in them, to distinguish what I know from what I know I do not know, and even to understand sufficiently much of what a scientist tells me. For example, I can understand what my doctor says and I can view my organism in a way sufficiently near to his way of viewing although, unlike today, my generation was taught no human biology unless they were biologists. I am conscious of winds and tides because I have sailed; but what I know about them I have read about to enlarge my understanding enough for my purposes. I am conscious of the water cycle because it excites my imagination. I am still more conscious of the oxygen cycle and, correspondingly, I am indignant at the threat to the Amazon jungle; yet I should score low marks in a paper designed to test my understanding of the mechanisms and transformations involved. What I do know I did not learn in school.

It is an occupational disease of academics that they hate not to teach their subject in depth. The late Lord Lindsay, when he established a university at Keele with a compulsory first-year general course, had in mind not only the widening of students' minds but, perhaps even more, the widening of the minds of the faculty. A physicist ought to be made to think out what a nonphysicist in this era needs to know about physics. Every discipline would be better, even when at home with its own specialists, for having thought out a program suitable for mere passers-by. Lord Lindsay has proved, I understand, a lesson that not all have been willing to learn. Was he asking too much, not of human nature, not even of Western culture, but of that preselected group to whom, because they are specialists, we entrust the general education of our intellectual elite?

I repeat — elite — chosen because of their ability to profit by higher education. Before they reject it, let English speakers reflect that in France — its native land — the word is still of good standing on the political left and connotes a world in which people are chosen for their ability to learn and to do, rather than by birth, wealth, or patronage. By what criteria do we choose this sector of our population? To what do we invite them to dedicate so many years of what is already young manhood? And to whom do we entrust their guidance during these precious years?

It is becoming common to criticize the criteria of selection for putting too great a premium on causal, as distinct from contextual, understanding, on analysis rather than synthesis. Brain science is beginning to make respectable a belief, which for many people is a fact of direct experience, that we have two

modes of understanding and that our scientific, though not our historical studies, tend to overrate the linear, analytical, and logical mode against the contextual and synthetic one. A case history clamors to be included.

In the early days of IQ testing, tests briefly became an English party
game. At one party our host said he would test our intelligences. He then read
quickly a number of disconnected statements about three men: a driver, a fireman, and a guard of a (steam) railway train whose names (but in no stated
order) were Jones, Smith, and Robinson. The last statement was "Smith beat
the fireman at billiards." Then came the question—"What was the name of the
engine driver?"

The fireman's name was not Smith. But so what? There were still three
possibilities for the driver. Two names must have been foreclosed by some
information derivable from that jumble of earlier statements but none of the
statements, except the last, had specifically attributed or excluded a name to or
from anyone. None the less, in the silence that followed, my wife immediately
and confidently said "Smith." The following dialogue ensued:

Host: You mean Smith was the name of the engine driver?
E: Of course.
Host: How did you do it so quickly?
E: Do what?
Host: Solve the clues.
E: What clues?
Host: (patiently but painfully explains what the clues were for)
E: Oh, I didn't understand all that.
Host: (totally puzzled) Then how did you know that the engine driver's
name was Smith?
E: (equally puzzled) But of course it would have been the engine
driver who was playing billiards with the fireman. They work on
the same foot plate, they belong to the same union. The guard is
at the other end of the train, a different union, a different pro-
motion ladder. He wouldn't even know the fireman.

(a pause, broken by increasing laughter)

Host: He might have.
E: I suppose. (a pause) But Smith *was* the name of the engine
driver, wasn't it?
Host: (glumly) Yes.

To my wife, an engine driver was an engine driver and a fireman was a
fireman. The rest of us had thrown away all the information included in the
context and treated these men as symbols A, B, and C. We knew what was
expected of us to show intelligence. She didn't.

I do not underrate the value of deductive processes when they can help to validate or correct contextual understanding; but they should not obscure contextual understanding. Historians are divided in the importance they attach to the contexts of human actors on the stage of history, but few would wholly ignore it and fewer are convincing when they do. Is there a difference, in this regard, between the humanities and the sciences? I think there is; but also in science, context can be powerful, both to enlighten and to blind. Michael Polanyi (1963) lived long enough to see a theory in the textbooks that he had put forward as a doctoral student forty years before. The evidence and the argument were unchanged. Nothing had changed except the intellectual climate, which had become sufficiently congenial to accommodate his insight.

What then is general education? My wife's knowledge of the division of duties on a steam-driven railway train was not derived from school or from experience in driving a train. It was common knowledge to the whole group, though only she chose to use it. Was she unusually gifted in contextual understanding or only unusually free from inhibitions in using it? Do some subjects encourage it more than others? Is it different from interdisciplinary or even transdisciplinary knowledge and skill?

To the implied criticism of postsecondary education for its failure to contribute to general education, there is one radical but serious answer. It can be said that formal general education stops and should stop at the end of secondary school (as in Germany) or even earlier (as in England). Thereafter, the student should be able to continue his general education for himself. Postsecondary education is necessarily specialized and those who impart it are necessarily specialists — specialists even more specialized than those whom they teach, since many of the students are would-be professionals who will be using more than one speciality. The problem of general education is indeed real, but it is a problem for primary and secondary school. Thus, its success is to be judged not only or chiefly by the spread of knowledge and skill that the students have acquired, but, primarily, by their ability and keenness to continue for themselves a search that will last as long as they live. There is no lack of books and other media to satisfy this search. There has probably never been a time when the inquiring mind was so well provided for outside the institutes of formal education. No formal institute is needed to meet the needs of general education beyond the age of eighteen, and if it were, it would have to be differently staffed and differently organized. Nor should it be expected to award any degree or certificate of any sort of expertise won.

This is a serious argument. It substantially describes the present situation, except that primary and secondary schools are still diverted from the task of general education by university requirements, which are irrelevant to most of their students. There are even some postsecondary colleges that approach the role described here for an alternative form of higher education.

It is even possible to describe the sort of general education that might emerge in such alternative establishments. It would be organized, not around disciplines or even around professions, but around problems. Why have a billion people gone Marxist in the last sixty years? What do we mean by human adaptability and what limits it? Or, to start even further up the scale, What are the issues that we should most like to better understand? In each inquiry, the perpetual censoring question would be — how *little* skill and knowledge need we acquire in this field in order to further our understanding of this particular complex situation, as it is defined by our multiple interests in it?

It is an exciting thought. There is probably a place for such establishments. But we should not readily agree to limit our universities to explicitly specialist roles for at least two reasons. First, the study of historical (but not specifically human) subjects has already defined some disciplines, notably ecology, in a way that does indeed call on a host of sciences and uses as little of each as it needs. It is problem-oriented almost by definition. The second reason is even more important. Might not even specialties be better taught if teachers saw the subject matter in the context of all the other specialties to which they contribute and which contribute to them? If so, the question raised is not so much the general education of the students as the general education of the faculty.

Faculty seminars are notoriously difficult to run, to keep going, and, even more, to keep growing. The dice are loaded against the faculty members who want to spend any of their time understanding their neighbor's field or explaining their own, even to a neighbor who wants to hear about it. This is not as true of the professional schools; but even they have their difficulties. I know a department of planning that wanted an economist. They could only hire such a person as a member of the department of economics. But as such, when the time came, they could not get their economist tenure, since the position had only been on loan to another department. How could his colleagues judge him as an economist?

And yet, are we to relegate these highly qualified persons to the status of pit ponies, condemned to work in the dark because that is where the coal is? I am not an academic; I do not know. I can imagine a better possibility only on two conditions, neither of which can be assumed as possible from any experience of mine.

One is that academics should become primarily teachers, absorbed by the excitement of passing on what they know and engaging interest; especially in what they do not know, but long to know, and believe to be knowable. The other is that they should discover that transdisciplinary teaching is as serviceable as more conventional teaching for the specific purpose of getting necessary grades and that it should come to be esteemed by students as well as teachers as more effective and more enjoyable than the more blinkered conventional approach.

Perhaps one principle may encourage us to believe in the possibility of the second condition. It is this: The way we arrange and expound some understanding that we have achieved is seldom the way in which we acquired it. The urge to tidy it up is hard to resist. Why keep the ladder standing when we have climbed it? It is hard to remember, even if we try, the route by which we have arrived. Yet those whom we wish to guide to the same place cannot skip those steps which cost us so much labor. They must come by the same route, although we may be able to speed their passage; and, as we look back, that route is by no means always the route that looks most logical to us.

Teaching can only be a guide to learning; it cannot be a substitute. Perhaps we would do better to speak of all educational establishments, not as places of teaching, but as places of learning. Viewed thus, it seems less improbable that less structured and less specialized teaching might result in quicker learning, even of the specialties.

The other difficulty remains. It is associated with the enormous prestige that has come to be associated with anything that can be called research — and published as research. It affects all the disciplines to some extent but especially the experimental and observational sciences. C. P. Snow (as he then was) in his famous lecture on the two cultures asserted that to any scientist, it would go without saying that the prime object of a university is to generate new knowledge. To any humanist, I think, it would seem equally obvious that the prime object of a university is to transmit the human heritage of skill and understanding — this overwhelming, ever-growing legacy, so easy to lose, so hard to recover, so precious an inheritance, and so weighty a responsibility for every member of each generation. For each of us must learn and transmit this knowledge as our generations turn over, three times in a century; and, for almost all of us, what we can add is trivial compared to what we can transmit — or lose.

This heritage is not a heap of elements. It is a synthesis — never stable and never complete — yet deriving its meaning from its interrelations. If this is not known to those who transmit the fragments, the burden will be greater on those who receive them and use them, and who, formally or informally, must play their part in passing them on.

Reference

Polanyi, M. "The Potential Theory of Adsorption." *Science,* 1963, *141* (3585), 1010–1013.

Sir Geoffrey Vickers is an English lawyer and administrator who has written and lectured extensively on the learning process. He is one of the visiting faculty of the Division for Study and Research in Education at the Massachusetts Institute of Technology and has been a Regent's Lecturer at the University of California at Berkeley.

*The subjects that make up a curriculum are usually taught falsely,
as if they were independent, although attention to context shows they
are not. Perhaps the best way of treating them together is by
emphasizing the categories that define them (as allocation and
distribution are economic categories), and then finding other
categories for the same material, thus moving to another subject.*

The Nature of
the Transdisciplinary:
An Elementary Statement

Ralph Ross

Education is a lifelong process in which we all share, constantly educating and
miseducating ourselves and others. Experience alone is no teacher; it can condition response but it cannot impart principles. That is reserved for reflection
as it plays on experience. Part of reflection is imagination, which is a native
capacity, like intelligence; it can be aided by education, but not given to those
who do not have it to begin with. Yet it can be disciplined so it becomes
responsible, and intelligence itself can be trained so that knowledge and wisdom can be derived from the materials of experience.

Schooling is what we have thought necessary to stock and train the
mind, and schooling has been done by subject matter. Basic to the schoolboy's
education, traditionally, are reading, writing, and arithmetic, the three Rs;
presumably because they are needed for more advanced study because they
are distinct subject matters like logic, grammar, and rhetoric, the medieval
trivium. But are they distinct? Reading and writing are aspects of one subject,
and it is impossible to teach writing without reading for, at the very least, one
must read what he wrote. Is arithmetic separate from reading and writing?
Whatever else can be said about their connection, all three are aspects of
thinking, at least insofar as arithmetic isn't taught by rote learning and

A. White (Ed.). *New Directions for Teaching and Learning: Interdisciplinary Teaching*, no. 8.
San Francisco: Jossey-Bass, December 1981

memorization. An unfortunate consequence of treating these three as distinct subjects is that talented children have been divided into those who can do literature and those who can do mathematics, with only a few who can do both. One result, on a large scale, has been the two cultures about which C. P. Snow worried. Indeed, there is still a literary-artistic culture with almost no comprehension of mathematics and science, and a scientific culture which, I think, does a little better, but not well, about understanding or, at least, accepting the virtue of a literary culture. Unfortunately, many people in the literary culture, aware that science underlies technology, blame science for the urban and rural blight that business uses of technology have brought us and for the mechanization and boredom of much work.

Examination of "subjects" studied at a later age shows that they are far from self-contained, despite the fact that they are treated as such and taught in isolation from each other. One may study literature, for example, and should see at once that history and philosophy, religion and manners are involved in what one reads. Without knowledge of ancient Greek burial customs and the devotion to chthonic deities, one can make only partial sense of Sophocles' *Antigone*. Without understanding something of the French Revolution, Napoleon's relation to it, reaction in France after Napoleon, doctrines of the Roman Catholic Church, and the role of the clergy under the restored monarchy, a reader will find Stendhal's *The Red and the Black* impenetrable. All this is obvious enough, for imaginative literature is about something other than itself, and it may therefore seem that literature is a special case. But is it?

The study of history is often the study of events in chronological order. The issue is: what kinds of events? If the answer given is "historical events," we are offered no help, for a historical event is only an event that occurred in the past, and for historians all events with which they deal are past events. Even if one recorded an event just as it was happening, by the time one finished recording it (by any means), the event would be past. The events of history are of all kinds, including literary events. If they were parceled out to different subject matters, all subject matters would be included, for everything has a history, from logic to marriage. And it is probably wise not to catalogue events under subject matters when one writes history, for there is no real political activity (as opposed to studies of what are called government or political science) apart from economics, no war apart from politics, and perhaps no economics (actual, not theoretical) apart from politics, or, although the words stick in one's throat, no politics apart from war or its possibility. Specialization in a subject, or even better, in one part of a subject, has yielded a quickening of knowledge, what has been called the knowledge explosion, and is pursued avidly both for the sake of knowledge and for the personal rewards involved; but specialization is also the fragmentation of mind and of subject matter. Sociology has been called the study of society. What, then, do political science, economics, and social psychology study? Clearly, parts of society. And if sociology omits those parts, how much of society is left for it? Not just crumbs from the table of other studies, but somehow not the whole loaf either, unless society is really studied as a whole. But, then, that would take a joint effort by all the social and behavioral sciences.

I shall deal later with what is required for such a joint effort. First, I want to call attention to the lack of sophisication of our studies, especially in the lower grades, despite the massive infusion of method in the higher grades. As an illustration of the application of method to subject matter, let us again consider the study of history. Children are usually taught history (next to English, it has always been the largest department in our schools) in a mechanical fashion, which may even involve the use of flash cards. The flash card technique has amusing implications. The teacher holds up a card on which is printed "1588" and the children are supposed to respond with the event of chief importance that took place in that year. The proper answer when I was in elementary school was "Drake defeated the Spanish Armada." The implication is that nothing else took place in 1588. In fact, the question was usually worded: "What happened in 1588?" So Sir Francis and the Spanish Armada battled while everyone else slept. It is only many years after this elementary training that a student asks himself what was meant by saying, for example, that Columbus discovered American in 1492. Columbus was not the first white man to arrive in America, if our knowledge of Norse exploration is adequate. But more startling, there were people here when Columbus arrived. Does this mean that only members of a certain race are allowed to discover things? Imagine the incredible arrogance of a man who arrives at a place where people live with a culture and a government of their own, and yet immediately plants a flag and says, "I claim this land in the name of the King of Spain."

At least as important as exploring the meaning of what is supposed to have occurred in the past is the problem of how anyone knows, in fact, that it did occur. Sentences in history textbooks are treated by uncritical teachers as if they were revelations attested to by the Deity. Yet, in fact, they are hypotheses, more or less probable, depending for their truth on a body of evidence. On examinations, the young student may be asked such questions as: "When did Caesar cross the Rubicon?" and his answer will be marked incorrect if it does not agree with the text. Evidence that makes us think we have the right date is rarely mentioned. Equally, students in biology classes may be asked if a whale is a fish, then marked incorrect if they answer yes because a whale is said to be *really* a mammal. A whale, of course, is not born with the sign "mammal" on his back; whales are classified as mammals rather than fish because, as we all know, zoologists find it more important to classify creatures in terms of traits such as the possession of mammary glands and vertebrae and the practice of suckling their young, than in terms of their natural habitat.

In history classes the teacher says, "Columbus discovered America," because, for certain purposes, it is important to consider the time at which Europe first became aware of the existence of that continent, but the sentence then means neither that Columbus was the first man in America, nor even the first white man.

The problem of verification, discovering whether or not a statement is true, has a special difficulty in the field of history. Actual history, the past itself, is over; historiography, the writing of history, is about the past. One cannot return to the past in order to discover whether or not what is said by historians is true. How, then, are we to discover the evidence for any historical statement? That evidence, like all evidence, exists in the present; it is composed of official documents, diaries, memoirs, obelisks, coins, and so on. The statements in history books are hypotheses about the past and depend for their truth on the adequacy of their interpretation of a mass of documentary material. History, as a scholarly discipline, is an attempt to discover the past by the use of materials existing in the present. Often, this is something that the student does not learn until he is in graduate school, and on the way to becoming a professional historian himself.

History, like all other studies, contains an enormous amount of classification that depends on the purposes of the historian. As these purposes change, and they do change constantly, the characteristic terms of history change with them. So, if preliterate man is said to have lived through certain stages, which at one time were described as nomadic, hunting and fishing, and agricultural, this means, not that these are the stages through which early man *really* lived (although it is not a sheer fabrication); but, in terms of an interest in the relation between man and the way in which he has earned a living, the historian has decided to use certain data about preliterate man for his classification, rather than other data in which he is not so interested. The historian's interest in this relationship is itself based upon a principle, probably implicit, to the effect that one can discover more things about people more easily if one knows, to begin with, how they earn their living. When, in somewhat later historical writing, preliterate man was said to have lived through an old stone age, a new stone age, a bronze age, and so on, this does not mean that the historian has discovered that people did not, in fact, win a living by successively hunting and fishing and later engaging in agricultural pursuits; but that something has changed today, not in the past, and the historian has adopted a new principle to the effect that it is more important to classify periods of human life by the tools people employ rather than by their occupations.

Elementary sophistication of this kind does not exist widely, even on the college level; but sophistication about the interdependence of what are called subjects, which dwell in departments as people dwell in apartments, and which, like the latter, are designed to be apart from each other, has been too rare in graduate schools. One reason for this is the sheer amount of knowledge that specialization yields. Another reason is that subjects have been defined so that they seem, and to some extent are, quite different from each other. When it becomes apparent that each subject needs context, provided by another subject, and that there are indispensable links of meaning, it becomes necessary to change the boundaries of each subject, at least for particular purposes, and that poses difficulties. Perhaps the problem is that we usually talk about subject matter, that aspect of the world that is studied by those who practice a subject, rather than the basic concepts they employ.

When we think of the categories, or basic concepts, of each study, we may even be able to deal with the question that has stopped transdisciplinary study in the past again and again as if it had run into an electrified fence. Put bluntly, the question is: Even if there is some virtue in interdisciplinary teaching, is there any way scholarship or academic research can be done on interdisciplinary material? The answer used to be a sheepish no because transdisciplinary materials were not a subject, but were made up of several subjects. The assumption was that a subject somehow circumscribed a part of the world and all studies of that part were made in the name of the subject. It was further assumed that the circumscribed bit was a kind of natural whole. Then, in interdisciplinary study, if one added still another such whole, one could talk about the two but could no more study them than one could study apples and oranges together, which cannot be added to make a genuine sum, but are forever apart arithmetically. Somehow it was not pointed out that if one studies apples and oranges together one is closer to learning about fruit than if one studies each separately.

Subjects are not wholes torn from the world to be studied in isolation. Nor are they experiences of a special kind with no relation to experiences of other kinds. Subjects are perhaps best understood as defined by categories, or basic concepts, in accordance with which we select the kinds of experience to which those categories are appropriate, and which will help us to organize and explain. Economic transactions, for example, are complicated psychological, social, and political phenomena that economists treat in such terms as price, production, allocation, and distribution. Political scientists treat the same phenomena with an entirely different set of concepts, which include legal ones. But, one may say, the transaction was "economic," and that gives economics some priority. No, there are no priorities, only interests. The actions that one person thinks of as economic may be thought of by another person as dramatic, perhaps a subject for a play; that is just as legitimate as treating it as economic, although neither excludes the other from someone's consideration. A particular action may be economically excellent, politically dangerous, and morally repulsive.

As one increases the categories one uses in thought, one increases the size of the object of thought. Finally, one deals with nature, society, and humanity, and one may go on to their relations. Indeed, one probably must: people must eat to survive, and their food comes from nature; they must at least gather the food, and by now they must produce it and it must be distributed. People must breathe the air and drink the water which must be pure enough for life. Humanity, nature, and society are all implicated at once. The problems of life are all transdisciplinary; only the problems of specialists are specialized. Emphases differ, of course. To overstate the case, but still within reason, by studying anything, we have an object of contemplation and we gain an esthetic satisfaction; by studying nature, we learn the nonhuman context of the human, including life itself; by studying society we learn the ways that institutions and cultures make men and women what they are; and by studying the humanities, we learn the ways that men and women make their institutions and cultures. Also, by studying nature and society, we learn the conditions of our values and the ways in which values mold us; by studying the humanities, we study the values themselves and appraise the worth of everything, including nature, society, humanity, and our studies of them.

I want to conclude with a few words about the humanities, which seem unfortunately to need a special defense today. Life in the twentieth century becomes ever more abstract and impersonal. The humanities, insofar as they are concerned with the arts, are, above all, concrete and personal. The arts and their study are the countervailing force to the dehumanizing tendencies of size, mechanization, and automation. Yet it is not enough merely to keep the human element alive in the midst of the artifacts of humanity and inhumanity. They are not an enemy to be opposed, but great creations of the human mind to be utilized for the purposes of humanity.

The categories of the social sciences are adapted to the world we live in; they help us explain human behavior in terms like status and role. Humanistic terms are different. Basic among them are person and conduct. It is a person, not a cipher, who enters different statuses, and each person's behavior is thought of as conduct when we recognize its moral quality. If we ask how sons in a particular society respond to the deaths of their fathers we may have a question for sociology and psychology. But if we ask how Hamlet responded to the death of his father, and Laertes to the death of his, and Fortinbras to his, we have a question for a poet.

Even the necessary abstractions and classifications of the social sciences tend to dehumanize, for abstractions in thought easily lead to impersonality in conduct. Consider the working class of the economists, the proletariat of the Marxists, those who sell their services for a wage. If a man thinks of himself as a member of the working class and joins a union or feels class solidarity, he *may* start to lose his identity as a person and so his special quality as a moral being. He becomes more faceless and less human.

Yet we are forced into dehumanizing patterns in work and thought, if we are to make the social machinery work. Mass production, for example, is only feasible if its products are almost identical, and any part of the product sufficiently like all other parts of the same sort to be interchangeable. A Ford carburetor for a particular model must be replaceable by any other Ford carburetor for the same model, with no loss of efficiency in performance. Interchangeability and replaceability are essential criteria for mass production. And what of the workers on the production line? As workers at a particular job, they perform virtually identical operations, may be interchanged (ideally with no loss in efficiency), and may be replaced if ill, old, or worn-out. In terms of status and role, and of economic function, workers on an assembly line must be judged by the same criteria we apply to the things they make. Yet as a person and a moral agent, the worker is still unique and irreplaceable. This is what the arts show us clearly.

We may learn much more about mankind, including strange things about the depths of the human soul, from the Karamazovs. But that is only possible because *The Brothers Karamazov* works properly as a novel, and so has fully individualized and unique characters—persons. Ivan Karamazov may be a symbol of the man of intellect, but he could not be an adequate symbol if he were only a symbol.

I have said that the humanities must not merely be a counter to the natural and social sciences. They must take their place in a pattern of knowledge that includes all sciences and all art. One way of making the pattern intelligible is to ask what science does that can yield so much power. The answer is that it discovers the conditions under which events occur. Then, if we can institute the conditions, we can bring about the events. We even learn sometimes under what conditions things and events disappear, and then control of the conditions allows us to eliminate the things or events. And if the social sciences can learn the conditions under which people do and don't do some things, we may have increased power over human action.

So the sciences give us a fulcrum to move the world, but if we do not use the fulcrum with care, we dislodge ourselves. What is the meaning and value of the events we can create or destroy? That is what the humanities study. The study of the arts and philosophy, the study of the arts as a way to philosophy, the study of history as one of the humanities (it is also science), can teach us what it is like to be human under a variety of conditions, and what it is like to experience what all humanity experiences. From the standpoint of knowledge, the humanities offer a complement to the sciences. The latter explain how things occur and the humanities explore the possible meanings and values of the things that do occur. From the standpoint of practice, the humanities offer a complement to the power science gives us, for they help us choose the ends for which we use power, the human goals we must never forget. In our technological age, in which the humanities may *seem* less relevant than they once were, they are more important than ever before, because we need them much more.

Ralph Ross is Hartley Burr Alexander Professor of Humanities and professor of Philosophy, Emeritus, Scripps College. He is the author, editor, or coauthor of seven books including Obligation, The Arts of Reading, The Fabric of Society, *and* The Philosophy of Edmund Burke, *and contributor to many scholarly journals.*

The twenty-fifth anniversary of the founding of the Society for General Systems Research is the occasion of some reflections on the difficulty of establishing interdisciplinary studies as illustrated by the present ambiguous position and possible future of the general systems enterprise.

The Future of General Systems

Kenneth E. Boulding

The Origin of General Systems

The Society for General Systems Research celebrated its twenty-fifth anniversary at an international meeting in London in August 1979. The meeting was a lively, controversial, and, at times, even heated occasion. It suggested that there was a lot of life in the middle-aged dog, that the potential of its ideas were by no means exhausted, and that it has a future. The occasion was of particular interest to me because I was one of the four founding fathers of the Society in 1954, along with Anatol Rapoport; the late Ralph Gerard; and the real founder of general systems, the late Ludwig von Bertalanffy. The occasion, therefore, was a suitable one for that mixture of nostaliga for the past and hopes of the future which an anniversary is supposed to evoke.

The foundation of a society is not, of course, the birth of an idea, but the production of a box to put the idea in, and certainly the idea of general systems goes back long before 1954. In the 1930s and 1940s, Einstein had pursued, without much success, the elusive concept of a unified field theory even in physics. Operations research emerged out of the Second World War—a set of techniques in model building, applicable to a very wide range of problems in many disciplines. Cybernetics also emerged after the Second World War as a set of theoretical concepts, again covering a very wide variety of disciplines. Model building expanded from econometrics, which really dates from the 1920s and 1930s, into other fields of social life. The rise of computers after the

A. White (Ed.). *New Directions for Teaching and Learning: Interdisciplinary Teaching*, no. 8. San Francisco: Jossey-Bass, December 1981

Second World War enormously expanded the ease with which complex models could be handled and projections made.

In its origin, the general systems movement, as reflected in the original Society for the Advancement of General Systems Theory (which later changed its name to the Society for General Systems Research) had no very grandiose designs. In the original manifesto, in the program for the American Association for the Advancement of Science for a meeting in Berkeley, California, in December 1954, a general system was defined as any theoretical system applicable to more than one of the traditional departments of knowledge. Interest in general systems, I think, came from two sources. The first was a feeling among practitioners in a number of different fields that any investigation of a practical problem of some system in the real world had to transcend the conventional disciplinary lines because the real world was not really divided according to the usual disciplines.

My own interest in general systems developed out of my study of the labor movement, in which it became very clear to me that at least all the social science disciplines had to be employed. A kind of practical problem-solving approach, whether in urban transportation, income maintenance, the study of crime and the apparatus of the law, or the theory of any aspect of public policy, inevitably required the utilization of many disciplines, including often the physical and biological sciences, particularly as applied to engineering, agriculture, health, pollution, and so on. The inability of the real world to be compartmentalized means that any kind of problem-solving activity requires an interest in the general system that underlies the problem and cannot be confined to any one discipline.

In the physical and biological sciences, a second approach has been more common. The movement toward greater generality took place mainly where the boundaries of one science impinged on the boundaries of another so that interstitial fields developed. Molecular biology was a spectacular example in the last generation. For a hundred years physical chemistry has shown a tendency to expand into each of its original components. Within the field of the life sciences, the old departments of botany and zoology tended to be swallowed up in a larger department of biology. It became clear that when one was considering the ecological sciences, all ecosystems involved both plants and animals, and, even in the study of genetics and of the growth of the phenotype, the distinctions between plants and animals are not all that significant. In meteorology it has become clear that what happens in the atmosphere cannot be isolated from biological and societal activity. There cannot, indeed, be any science of self-contained, isolated systems or else we would never be able to find out about it. A science is always a product of the interaction between some system and the scientist or the scientific community and some part of its environment. Not even physics can exist in the absence of a physicist!

Curiosity about General Patterns of the Universe

Somewhere between the urgency of practical problems and the inner dynamics of scientific enterprise is idle curiosity, the pure itch to know, and this again is an important component of the general systems enterprise. The search for the unity of human knowledge comes from the faith, perhaps a little blind, in the fundamental unity of the real world and its inescapable interconnectedness. General systems has always been very cautious about trying to find a general system of practically everything. Nevertheless, the itch for unification is there and it is hard to avoid scratching it a little. I must confess to having felt and scratched this itch more, perhaps, than most general systems buffs, but always a little hesitantly, feeling the danger of too much monism in a universe with such enormous diversity and complexity, and being constitutionally unsympathetic toward the naive reductionism that sought to reduce everything to the crude simplicities of physics or of the material world. There is also a hankering for useful simplifications; maps and charts and patterns that would at least illuminate the unfamiliar with the distant glow of familiarity, and guide us to the vast uncertainties and unknowns of a rather frightening future.

Two patterns impress themselves on me by their universality. One is the pattern of the history of an entity from its beginning to its end, from the initial creation of its potential to the final exhaustion of that potential, whether a mountain range, a living organism, or a social organization. The other pattern has been the interaction among entities, species, in the ecosystems and in the irreversible ongoing patterns of evolution.

The first pattern is the physiology of the creodic path, as Waddington (1960) called it. It starts with an "origin" in terms of erogeny or mountain building, the fertilized egg of a biological organism, the founders of an organization, a religion, or a country. Then follows the realization of that potential through time, as affected by successive environments and by the internal necessities of the development of structure. James Miller's (1978) nineteen substructures of a living organism is an extraordinary example of a general systems taxonomy, even though we still have to explain growth, development, and eventual decay.

The Evolutionary Process

The other side of the coin is the interaction of entities, species, and populations in ecological systems, producing that irreversible change through mutation and selection that constitutes evolution. Evolution, indeed, I have defined as ecological interaction under conditions of constant change of parameters; ecological interaction being selection, and the change in parameters being mutation. Contemplating the evolutionary process from the "big bang" to the space shuttle, one perceives an important system principle: that systems themselves change in a systematic way, producing the perception of systems of the second order, that is, a system of change of systems. We see this very clearly in the evolutionary process where evolution itself evolves, that is, the process itself changes, as one process realizes its potential.

The process of prebiological evolution of the elements, the compounds, the stars, and other entities through the cosmological universe tends to follow principles of internal dynamics and phase transitions without very much ecological interaction, though I am not sure about this. How much, for instance, the production of the chemical elements, compounds, stars, and planets is a result of the ecological interaction of different elements, compounds, and structures, I do not know. As soon as we get something like catalysis into this process, however, something like an ecological system emerges. The population of the substance that is produced by catalysis and the populations of the things that produce it are obviously affected by the population of catalysts. The operations of catalysis still seem to be a little mysterious, but the catalyst seems to form something resembling a template that perhaps attracts atoms of different kinds and forces them into a close association, which produces chemical union. Something like this could presumably take place even in liquid or gaseous environments; for instance, an increase in the number of large molecules might push smaller molecules, atoms, or radicals into unions that otherwise might not happen.

Another possible source of structure formation is Prigogine's "far from equilibrium" dissipative systems in chemical reactions that produce structures by a dynamic process involving probabilistic events producing "births" or "deaths" of particular chemical structures (Nicolis and Prigogine, 1977).

This leads us into "autopoiesis," the systematic pattern of development of more complex structures out of less complex structures, the theory of which has been developed so elegantly by Zeleny (1980). Autopoietic processes are those in which a system has a potential for events with varying degrees of probability. When one of these events actually happens (and no matter how low the probability of anything, if we wait long enough it will come off), the probability of neighboring events in the system is changed. Depending, of course, on how these probabilities have changed, the system moves toward various kinds of order. This is really a theory of the instability of chaos. Systems of this kind undoubtedly appear at prebiological level, and they may be of great importance at the biological level too, but it is not easy to identify them.

With the development of DNA and life, evolution goes into a very different gear. DNA is a chemical structure coding an enormous amount of information and possessing very extraordinary properties. It is capable of self-reproduction by a kind of super self-catalysis. It is further capable of organizing a process of production, that is, a life history of a phenotype or organism. DNA has not merely information, it has "know-how." The fertilized egg in which I originated "knew how" to make me, it did not know how to make a black female. It did not have the slightest idea how to make a hippopotamus, though it did know how to make a skeleton, heart, liver, lungs, brain, and so on which at least have some family resemblance to the corresponding organs of the hippopotamus.

With the development of life, ecological interaction suddenly rises to great importance in the selective process. Selection is the process by which populations of different species rise, fall, or find an equilibrium level at which they are neither rising nor falling. A population rises if the additions exceed the subtractions and falls if the subtractions exceed the additions. The additions come from birth and in-migration; the subtractions from death and out-migration. These four variables will be a function of the population itself, and if the functions are such that there is an equilibrium population, this is the "niche" of the species and the species is viable. These niches are expanding or contracting all the time, as the parameters of the system change. When the niche shrinks to zero, the population becomes extinct. All ecosystems have "empty niches," that is, species which would have an equilibrium in the ecosystem if they existed. Thus, before rabbits and European-type humans were introduced, Australia clearly had an empty niche for them.

The evolutionary process consists essentially in the filling of empty niches either by mutation or by migration. It is not a deterministic process, simply because the probability of filling an empty niche is always less than 1.0; if it is not filled before it closes, as all niches eventually will because of changes in other parts of the system, the whole subsequent history of the system is different. Nevertheless, there may be autopoietic principles at work here. In something like emergent evolution, an empty niche, or something like it, may be filled from different directions. The most famous example of this was the evolution of the eye, by very different routes, in both mammals and the octopus. The principle here seems to be that if there is a good idea, somebody is likely to have it; but who that somebody is may be a little random. If it is a very good idea, more than one somebody may have it.

Societal Evolution

With Adam and Eve, or Homo and Mulier sapiens, evolution went into another phase or "gear change," this time in the production of human artifacts. The key factor here is the extraordinary capacity of the human brain to "know-what" as well as "know-how," that is, to develop internal images of the world that have some one-to-one correspondence or mapping with the real world outside. Know-how can be developed without very much know-what. Thus, a fertilized egg has a great deal of know-how, but probably no know-what at all. Similarly, a tennis player may have a great deal of know-how as to how to hit a tennis ball without any know-what about differential equations of the second and third degree, coefficients of elasticity, air resistance, and all the other things that determine the path of a ball that is hit by a racket. The rise of human folk technology, in terms of the making of flint arrowheads; the development of agriculture; the domestication of livestock; or the development of weaving, pottery, basketry, metallurgy, and so on, is mostly know-how, though a subtle know-what develops slowly in observation of mechanics, the measurement of time, navigation, and so on.

With the rise of science in the last 500 years, however, the know-what of the human race has increased enormously, and this has led to a correspondingly large increase in know-how. Alchemists, who got the elements wrong, could never have produced plastics, and did not even succeed in producing gold. In the history of the human race, there have been many blind alleys leading to false know-what that did not produce know-how.

Human artifacts are as much a part of the world ecosystem as are biological artifacts. They are produced by processes that have a strong resemblance to biological production, in the sense that all production starts from some kind of know-how, a genetic factor, which then captures energy and transmits information in order to select, transport, and transform materials into the improbable shapes of the product of phenotype. Biological production never moved much beyond two sexes, and the genetic know-how is itself contained in the product, that is, in the phenotype. In the case of the production of human artifacts, the genetic components are contained in other artifacts, in fact, a wide range of artifacts, and production is multi-parental. The selective processes are rather similar in both cases. In the case of human artifacts, demand, that is the ability of a human artifact to satisfy the wants of those who are willing and able to buy it, is a very important factor in survival, and indeed, it is now an increasingly important factor even in the survival of biological organisms.

Human knowledge and valuations can also be seen as species in the larger ecosystem and subject to the same kind of evolutionary processes. Mutation, in this case, consists of new ideas, new valuations, which constantly are being produced in the enormous creative turmoil of the human brain. These are always subject, however, to the selective process, and, as in the biosphere, not many of them survive. Most mutations, indeed, are adverse. The few that are not proceed to change the future.

The Future Niches for General Systems

Looking at the general systems enterprise from an evolutionary perspective, we can ask ourselves, are there empty niches for general systems in various forms, are these likely to expand or contract, and how far is general systems itself likely to adapt to potential niches? Certainly in the first twenty-five years of the history of the Society for General Systems Research, the niche seems to be rather small. The membership of the society has hovered between 1,000 and 2,000. Between ten and twenty universities around the world have something that resembles a program in general systems. Courses in it are really quite rare. I know of no endowed chair in general systems, though there are some research institutes in which the name "systems" appears, such as the International Institute of Applied Systems Analysis in Vienna, and systems institutes of different kinds in some of the socialist countries. There is a potential Ph.D. in "Systems Science" at the University of Louisville. The *International Journal of General Systems* comes out of the program at SUNY in Binghamton, New York. All this is reminiscent of small coastal settlements on a large continent. The question being, of course, is the continent really there? Even if it is really there, are the obstacles to settlement too severe?

Perhaps the greatest obstacle to the expansion of general systems, particularly in the intellectual-academic community, is precisely the fact that, in part, gave rise to it—that the disciplines are the strongest unit in both the academic and professional communities, and they are suspicious of anything that seems to erode their boundaries. This is true even of philosophy, where there surely should be a place for general systems. On the whole, however, philosophers have been fairly hostile toward it, seeing it as an amateur threat to professional interest. Unless, therefore, general systems itself becomes a discipline and an intellectual species, the other species in the intellectual ecosystem are likely to regard it more as a virus that threatens them than as a food to sustain them. Then, however, general systems will become a discipline of its own and it will be in danger of losing its generality. Indeed, this is already happening. The identification of general systems with systems science and especially with large-scale computer modeling may threaten its philosophical growing edges, even though systems science itself has a great deal of validity as a discipline.

There might be a niche, absurd as it may sound, for general systems as a kind of quasi-masonic order, a quasi-secret society, among those who have to be good little disciplinary boys and girls outside the lodge in order to survive, but who have a hankering for a larger view, a broader perspective than can be found in single departments or disciplines. Then general systems itself can sustain a discipline that can select out plausible nonsense and recognize even implausible truth. Indeed, the systems practitioners, while they may be critical with the narrowness of the disciplines, must not deny the importance of discipline itself, that is, the process by which the detection of error can be rewarded. The greatest contribution of general systems to the disciplines could be to show that its discipline is itself inadequate and will fail to detect error, if the disciplines are too self-contained and too much closed to information from the outside.

I am optimistic enough to believe that there is a bias in the evolutionary patterns of the universe running toward complexity and control and also toward truth. The "time's arrow" of evolution toward organizations of greater complexity, more elaborate control in cybernetic systems, and a greater capacity for internal images of the external world that could be called intelligence, has many puzzling features. It seems to come, however, from the fact that ecosystems are more likely to have empty niches at the top than at the bottom;

34

that is, for organizations of higher complexity, control, and intelligence, simply because the niches at the bottom are more likely to be already filled. Similarly, within the great ecosystem of the human mind, the innumerable species of erroneous images are likely to be less stable than species of true images, simply because error can be found out and truth cannot.

If there are indeed general patterns of the universe, however complex the systematic structure, then the images that deny the possibility of such a pattern are in error and are likely to be more unstable than those that affirm it. Of course, to affirm the possiblity of a pattern is not the same thing as discovering it, and perhaps the pattern may be forever inaccessible because of the limitations of image-forming potential. However, if we decide not to look for such a pattern, the chances of finding it are much diminished. The American continent, after all, existed long before Columbus, and, as some cynic said, how could Columbus miss it? Still, if nobody had believed it was worthwhile to sail west, there would have been no Columbus. This reflection gives me some optimism about the future of general systems.

References

Miller, J. *Living Systems*. New York: McGraw-Hill, 1978.
Nicolis, G., and Prigogine, L. *Self-Organization in Nonequilibrium Systems: From Dissipative Structures to Order Through Fluctuations*. New York: Wiley-Interscience, 1977.
Waddington, C. H. *The Ethical Animal*. London: Allen and Unwin Ltd., 1960.
Zeleny, M. (Ed.). *Autopoiesis, Dissipative Structures, and Spontaneous Social Orders*. Boulder, Colo.: Westview Press, 1980.

Kenneth E. Boulding was the first president of the Society for General Systems Research, and he was president of the American Association for the Advancement of Science in 1979. He is Distinguished Professor of Economics and a program director in the Institute of Behavioral Science at the University of Colorado, Boulder. His latest work on systems is Ecodynamics: A New Theory of Societal Evolution *(Beverly Hills, Calif.: Sage, 1978).*

Whereas physical order reflects underlying physical laws, biological and esthetic order result from a cyclic process of variation and selection.

Sketch for a Theory of Order

David Layzer

A snow crystal, an insulin molecule, a Bach chorale, and a painting by Mondrian are all nonrandom assemblages of simpler components — water molecules, amino acid residues, musical tones, and colored rectangles. Do the kinds of nonrandomness these structures exhibit have anything in common? Is the geometric order of the Mondrian more closely related to the order of a crystal or to that of, say, a Rembrandt portrait? Is an insulin molecule orderly in the same way as a crystal, or as a Rembrandt portrait, or as neither? Do different kinds of esthetically pleasing order — that of the Bach chorale and the Mondrian, for example — have anything in common?

I should like to sketch a theoretical framework for discussing questions like these. I shall argue that there are two basic kinds of order, *physical order* and *functional order*. The orderly structure of the snow crystal is purely physical. The insulin molecule, the Bach chorale, the Mondrian, the Rembrandt all exhibit, in diverse ways, functional order.

The distinction I shall draw between physical and functional order may remind some readers of Bergson's distinction, in *Creative Evolution*, between "geometric" and "vital" order. Bergson, too, would have put the snow crystal in the first category and the remaining examples in the second. He, too, argued, as I shall, that the second kind of order is produced either by biological evolution or by closely analogous "creative" processes. Bergson believed, however, that such creative processes do not admit rational analysis. He argued that human intelligence has been shaped by evolution to perceive and analyze geo-

A. White (Ed.). *New Directions for Teaching and Learning: Interdisciplinary Teaching,* no. 8.
San Francisco: Jossey-Bass, December 1981

metric order, as the eye has been shaped to sense and analyze light. I shall argue that the functional order, though different from physical order, is no less susceptible to rational analysis.

Another important difference between the theory I shall sketch and Bergson's concerns *disorder*. Bergson denied its existence. He argued that geometric order and vital order are complementary aspects of the world. The absence of one implies the presence of the other. We perceive disorder when we expect to find one kind of order and are confronted by another. Thus, a cluttered and untidy desk is not, according to Bergson, less orderly than one on which papers and books are arranged in neat piles: It is merely orderly in a different way. In contrast to this view, I shall argue that functional order supplements, rather than complements, physical order. The absence of functional order is not physical order but randomness. Functional order is absent in the snow crystal, present in the insulin molecule.

Physical Order

Physical order has its origin in physical laws. Thus, the orderly structure of atoms, molecules, and crystals is fully explained by quantum mechanics. Physical laws do not, however, wholly determine the structure of physical systems. Although the growth of a snow crystal is governed by quantum mechanical laws, the final product depends on the temperature and humidity that prevailed while the crystal was growing. The enormous variety of snow crystals shows that this dependence is very sensitive, while their perfect hexagonal symmetry show that the same conditions (at least the six free ends of the growing crystal) always produce the same kind of growth. Thus, every snow crystal preserves a record of the environment in which it grew.

What is true of the growth of snow crystals is true of all physical processes: They are governed by laws but depend also on initial and boundary conditions. The laws give rise to physical order; the initial and boundary conditions may or may not be orderly. Those that determine the growth of a snow crystal vary in an essentially random way; hence the endless variety of snowflakes. Those that determine the sequence of amino acid residues in an insulin molecule, on the other hand, are clearly nonrandom, since they always (or nearly always) generate the same structure. What is the nature of this nonrandomness?

Biological Order

The unique sequence of amino acid residues in an insulin molecule does not have a physical or chemical explanation. The twenty amino acids that make up the alphabet of proteins can be joined in any order to form a peptide chain of any length, just as the letters of the English alphabet can be joined in any order to form a "word" of arbitrary length. But just as the vast majority of such "words" are meaningless, so the vast majority of theoretical possible peptide chains are biologically meaningless, that is, functionless. And the meaning (function) of each meaningful (functional) chain is distinct from that of every other. I suggest that biological order consists in this specificity of function.

The concept of function has no place in physics, but it is central in biology. If you ask a physicist what determines the shape of an insulin molecule, he will say: the sequence of amino acids. If you now ask — Why that particular sequence? — he will probably reply that the question has no meaning for him as a physicist; the amino acid sequence is a matter of initial conditions, and physicists do not worry about initial conditions.

A biologist, on the other hand, will explain that the amino acid sequence has been selected in the course of biological evolution because the shape of the resulting molecule enables it to perform a specific biological function: to recognize and bind to a specific receptor in the plasma membrane. (The attachment of an insulin molecule to the membrane of a fat or muscle cell makes it easier for glucose and certain other molecules to enter that cell.)

Although function is not a physical concept, it is neither subjective nor anthropomorphic. Changes in molecular function directly affect the fitness (expectation of reproductive success) of the organism in which they occur. To say that the insulin molecule is optimally adapted to its function means that no change in its sequence of amino acids can improve the organism's expectation of reproductive success.

The amino acid sequence of a protein is specified by a segment of DNA. Through natural selection, those DNA sequences that code for proteins that function best spread most rapidly in the population. Thus, the functional order of the insulin molecule is generated by the three fundamental processes of biological evolution: replication, genetic variation, and selection.

Functional Order in Works of Art

Let us pursue the analogy between protein molecules (or the segments of DNA that code for them) and concatenations of English letters. In this analogy, function corresponds to meaning: A functional protein corresponds to a meaningful word. The function of a protein, like the meaning of a word, depends to a greater or lesser extent on its context. Just as a word that is appropriate in one context may be inappropriate in another, so a protein that functions well in one biological context may function poorly in another. The biological context is defined by the genome as a whole and by the environment. We may compare the genome to a poem and the environment to a reader of the poem. Just as the fitness of a genome depends on the environment, so the meaning of a poem depends on the reader. And just as changes in the DNA sequences coding for individual proteins change the fitness of a genome (in a particular environment), so changes in individual words change the meaning of a poem (for a particular reader).

The meaning of a poem depends not only on the meaning of its individual words but also on how the words are combined in phrases, the phrases in clauses, and so on. Analogously, a genome specifies a hierarchically structured program of development. Besides segments of DNA that specify the amino acid sequences of proteins, there are DNA sequences that regulate and coordinate protein synthesis in ways that depend on specific features of the cellular environment. These parts of the genome contribute to fitness and evolve by natural selection just as the structural genes do. Analogously, the author of a poem selects not only the individual words but also the semantic and phonological structures in which they are embedded.

The evolution of a biological adaptation or a set of interdependent adaptations may be compared to the evolution of a poem from first draft to final version. The poet constructs successively "fitter" versions by inventing variants and selecting the "fittest." The impression of organic unity in a well-constructed poem — the impression that every word and phrase is uniquely determined by its context — arises in the same way as the unity of a biological organism and represents the same kind of order.

How valid is the analogy between fitness (expectation of reproductive success) and "fitness" (esthetic value)? At first they may seem to have little in common. Fitness is objective, "fitness" subjective. But this difference, I suggest, is not as fundamental as it may seem. The fitness of a genome depends on the environment. Because organisms tend to select favorable environments, the environmental range that a given population actually encounters is always a tiny and unrepresentative sample of the set of possible environments. Nevertheless, we may usefully focus attention on fitness differences relative to this narrow range. Analogously, in discussing the esthetic value of a piece of music, we may confine our attention to the judgments of people who are familiar with the particular musical idiom in which the piece is written. And such judgments are remarkably consistent. Everyone who listens to Baroque music agrees that Bach's chorales are superior to other harmonizations of the same tunes by less well-known composers of the same period. Everyone agrees that Mozart's duos for violin and viola are superior to those of Haydn, written at the same time in the same idiom, and that the original version of Brahms's B major piano trio is not as good as the revised version. Even though none of us is fully aware of the criteria underlying such esthetic judgments, the judgments themselves seem to be stable and widely shared.

Functional order is closely related to specificity. Suppose that N variants of a certain molecule are equally effective (in a given range of environments) in performing a certain function, and that, in the course of evolution, this class differentiates into smaller subclasses of molecules adapted to more specialized functions. The decrease in the number of molecules functionally equivalent to a given molecule represents an increase in functional order. Analogously the number of "esthetically equivalent" versions of a poem, a painting, or a piece of music diminishes as the composition "takes shape" —

becomes more orderly. In the end, the artist may be unable to change a single word, note, or line without diminishing the order he perceives in his composition.

Functional Order and Information

Information is a measure of functional order. Let N denote the number of possible peptide chains whose length does not exceed some fixed value. (The number of possible chains of length m is 20^m.) How much information is needed to specify the functional order of a given chain? Let n denote the number of chains whose fitness is equal to or greater than that of a given chain (for a given population and a given environmental range). I propose to measure the molecule's functional order by the quantity $\log(N/n)$. This quantity assumes its maximum value, $\log N$, when $n = 1$, that is, when any change in the molecule's amino acid sequence would reduce its fitness. At the other extreme, $\log(N/n) = 0$ when $n = N$, which will be the case when the molecule is nonfunctional.

Natural selection promotes the increase of functional order in a population, because genomes with small values of n (hence large values of $\log(N/n)$) reproduce more successfully than genomes with large values of n. Genetic variation increases *potential* functional order if (and only if) it gives rise to some genomes whose expectation of reproductive success exceeds that of existing genomes of the population.

The formula $I = \log(N/n)$ may be taken to define *functional information*. According to this definition, the functional information associated with a given structure is equal to the negative logarithm of the probability n/N that a structure picked at random from a population of variants will equal or surpass it, as judged in the light of some stable (but not necessarily explicit) criterion.

A work of art defines — admittedly not very precisely — its own class of variants. Thus, the variants of a Shakespearian sonnet must not only satisfy the usual prosodic constraints. They must also be recognizable as versions of the same sonnet. The metric structure and rhyme scheme, though not themselves aspects of functional order, help the poet to create functional order and the reader to apprehend it by helping to define a class of variants.

David Layzer is Donald H. Menzel Professor of Astrophysics at Harvard University. His research centers on cosmology, but he has also published theoretical papers on biological evolution and population genetics. He teaches two full-year, interdisciplinary courses in Harvard's core curriculum, "Space, Time, and Motion" and "Chance, Necessity, and Order."

*What is the basis for ethics, and what is the relation between ethics
and planning? How has this relation been expressed
in higher education?*

Gown and Town:
Planning Our Lives

C. West Churchman

In the truth seeker's life, uncertainty is pervasive. There is no such thing as a
truly good experiment. Every experiment I ever did or heard about, and that
includes those in the "hard" sciences as well as the "soft," has uncertainty
threaded through it. You can't avoid it. Since we are in that posture of being
uncertain about what we say, we have to make a value judgment. We have to
say, "All right, I've gone this far in trying to reduce uncertainty. I now think I
am in the position to make an approximate statement about the truth." At
best, all we can do is to *approximate* true statements. This means we must have
a value assumption basic to our statement. We think we have ascertained the
uncertainties accurately enough so that we can make a statement. We do that
as a community; we do not do it individually. We say that we, as a community, are willing to say that at this level this seems to be approximately the
case. We try to realize the value implications of making approximations.

I found in the 1940s what I really wanted to study and spend the rest of
my life on was planning. And that is what I have been doing since about 1945.
I call it the design of social systems, the connectedness theme in which all of
us, no matter where we are in this life, are interested. Pervading all of our lives
is the desire to try to improve our own individual life, that of our friends, that
of our family, that of our community, and so on.

The problem does have an intellectual side. We can call that side, in

A. White (Ed.). *New Directions for Teaching and Learning: Interdisciplinary Teaching,* no. 8.
San Francisco: Jossey-Bass, December 1981

compliance with the title of this chapter, the Gown. Gown is the intellectual side of designing Town. And by Town, I mean the life of us all in our individual lives, in families, in communities, and nations. The intellectual side of that effort to design our lives depends mainly on reason, intuition, and experience — and, most especially, that elusive function called judgment, which is some combination of all of the other three plus just plain human common sense.

Of course, this effort also has a humanist side, and especially a moral base as well as an esthetic one; so that everyone everywhere is a social systems designer. And, what connects us all, is that we are designers of our own lives. The designing goes on until we are dead. As far as I know, it may go on after that, and it may be that there should be some time devoted to the design of our afterlives.

Now, our central concern in the design of lives is ethics, though we are never quite sure what that means. We do know that one ethical aspect of designing a life is moral concern for future generations. We are coming to realize more and more, I hope, in the latter part of the twentieth century, that one of the biggest problems we have is to design a society where people in the future will find it easier, or at least more satisfactory and uplifting, to design their lives. Well, then, why do they, the future generations, have to cope with all the garbage that we seem to be generating to make their lives more difficult?

But I also think we are engaged in trying to design our lives to serve the dead, those who came before us. I believe that you should not be forced to give up your membership in humanity just because you happen to die. My students are always impressed by saying, "Now we have got to worry about the future." I say, "Wait until you have to worry about the past." They say, "What does that mean? The past isn't around anymore." I keep trying to tell them that when I pass on, I do not want all my expectations, hopes, and beliefs to simply disappear.

I have found that some of the best designers are not academics, nor have they any college degrees. You do not really need a college degree to be an excellent life designer. But, since I am an academic, I am interested in what things Gown has discovered by designing Town. Usually, these are expressed by Gown as principles or theories that aid the design. One of the characteristics of a truly Gown-approach to the design of social systems, however, is that we question principles, even the one I have just stated.

First of all, we are finding out more and more that the social systems we live in are strongly nonseparable. Nonseparable means that whatever happens in one segment of the social system, matters a great deal and has a great deal of influence on what happens in another segment. You cannot break up the social system you are dealing with into segments and say, "OK, over here you do this job and over there you do that job and there you do another job," and expect that you have a good design. What happens in the Department of the Interior with respect to parks has much to do with what happens in the Department of the Interior with respect to wildlife. Why then do we have two sections of the Interior Department — Wildlife and Parks? And what happens in the Bureau of Reclamation (still in the Department of the Interior) has a great deal to do with what happens to both the Parks and Wildlife Service. And so it goes. The federal government of the United States, in the main, is a fragmented organization. It tries as best it can to keep its tasks separate. At one time in my life I was interested in how the new earth-resource satellite was going to affect international relations. Where, I asked, does the project belong? It doesn't belong in the State Department because the State Department has nothing to do with the technical satellites that NASA put up in the sky, nor does it belong in NASA because it is international. So the project never got under way, not because it was unimportant or badly designed, but because the federal government simply could not hold it. It simply had to fall through the cracks.

Now, think of a college. Over here you have to teach these kids to write better, and over here you have to do some engineering learning, and over here you have to do some business administration learning, and so on. Each one of the different departments on the campus is given the task of learning for the students as if there were no connections. If you get through History I, OK; you got through History I. Never mind that that course may be highly important to a lot of other things you are going to do. Piece by piece we fill you up. The social systems designers have been learning over and over again that the fragmentation of organizations usually has a very bad effect on such matters as education of the young. It isn't that I am interdisciplinary in spirit, but anti-disciplinary. I really think that we ought to jump back over the nineteenth century, and in a reactionary fashion, redesign colleges the way it was done in the eighteenth century, pretty much free of disciplines. I mean, I have a picture of what would happen to Immanuel Kant if he came in to have an interview with a contemporary college dean. The dean would say to him, "Look, Immanuel, you've been caught piddling around with astronomy, and you've been into psychology and epistemology, and now I find out you're interested in sociology and ethics. I really think you're spreading yourself too much. Perhaps instead of three critiques, you could just confine yourself to one."

So my first principle is: It is as important to understand the interconnectedness of aspects of a system as it is to understand the aspects themselves. The second principle is: Whenever a problem involves helping a large number of people, or one person in a very difficult situation in his life, it helps to try to seek avenues of improvement by searching for the resources that already exist in the masses. The implications of this principle for college teaching is that the students know a lot, and we, the teachers, often fail to make use of that knowledge. There is a strong tendency to believe that the students are in no position to be able to judge where they should go for their learning, and that arriving at a design has to be done mainly through a counselor. When I was in the philosophy department at Wayne State University, the head of the department decided on his own that no student could take philosophy until his junior year.

Now where did he come to such a precise design of a learning life, applicable to all students, namely, that only after exactly 2.0 years were you ready to take on the learning of philosophy? Students know when they need philosophy. He succeeded in keeping many of them out because, after they went through the gorgeous gateway to their junior year, they were required to take his course. That resulted in something like five majors in philosophy out of 18,000 students.

The sources are there among the students, and we need somehow to try to find them. To the extent possible — and it is a large extent — students, no matter what their age, should be designing their own learning.

I come now to ethics. I have a bias or conviction about the intellectual attempt to understand the basis of ethics. In the 1780s two men wrote simultaneously, neither one knowing about the other, about the basis of ethics. Both of their books began with statements similar to: "The very basis of ethics is . . . ." In the case of Jeremy Bentham, the ethical principle was the greatest pleasure for the greatest number, which we have translated today, some two hundred years later, to mean that the basis of all ethics is economics in its broadest sense. The greatest pleasure of the greatest number turns out, later on, to be the greatest economic utility for the greatest number. In other words, Bentham said that we, as humans, are struggling to apply the ethical principle of affluence of resources available to each one in society. There have been various forms of Bentham's ethical principle since then that have tried to clarify what he was talking about.

Kant, on the other hand, was writing similarly but his basis was not the greatest pleasure for the greatest number; but rather what he called the moral law, which has no conditions attached. It is not an "If you want to do so and so, then you ought to do so and so." It is "Look, you ought to do so and so." I remember a friend of mine who said to me, "West, I'm planning to do some decision-making experiments, and since I can't get enough money to reinforce the subjects, what about applying electric shock to those who don't do well?" I said, "No." And he said, "Why not?" And I said, "Because it's morally wrong." He wanted to ask, "Why is it morally wrong?" I simply used Immanuel Kant's "Because it is." Kant went a little further, of course. He called his moral law the categorical imperative, called "categorical" because there were no ifs, ands, or buts about it. This moral law was, "So act that you can will the principle of your action to be a universal law." "Will" is important in that statement. Never will an act on a principle that cannot be willed to be universal.

Kant translated the categorical imperative into the statement, "Never act so as to treat humanity, either in yourself or another, as means only, but as an end withal." Unfortunately, I think this version has been a largely neglected principle among the intellectuals. The books that are coming out on ethics are still emphasizing the Benthamite principle and not the Kantian. For example, economists use "willingness to pay" as one of their basic ways to evaluate recreational programs within the Park Service. How much are you willing to pay in order to recreate in Yosemite Valley? Kant's principle states that the ethics of whether or not you come here is not based on your willingness to pay, but rather on the question, are you treating humanity *in yourself* as means only? This part of his clause is just as important as the other: "Are you treating humanity in others as means only?"

In my experience in social systems design, I have found system after system designed in such a way that people are treated exactly as machines are treated. For example, if your automobile has brake problems, you take it to the garage, they put in some new brake pads, and away you go. The medical model does the same thing. If you have a serious pain in the belly, you go to the doctor, he does something, and off you go again.

Do we treat students in our colleges in the same way? I do not know how to treat them; but come to Berkeley during registration week. Our principle is that a student waiting in a line will be serviced in a certain manner. The cost of the student's waiting is zero. It is only the server's cost that is calculated. We know on principle in a social systems design that a system managed in that way will have very long waiting lines, and, indeed, that is exactly what happens. The hypothesis is beautifully verified because we are treating the students mainly as means only; namely, as machines. Who is right? Bentham, who deals with the outside world and the environment (helps us to be sheltered, fed and clothed, and to have automobiles, television sets, and entertainment); or Kant, who worried about the inner life, the life of your soul (he called it "will"). Who is constantly seeking for equity? I do not think you can answer that question. It is an eternal dialectic that goes on, but what, unfortunately, has been happening in much planning and policy making is the neglect of the Kantian principle.

Now, we come to another aspect of social systems design. Over the years, we have learned that imagination and intuition are very, very important, and that we need not be afraid of using this elusive function that we all have and that we call imagination. We have come to distinguish between two kinds of social systems design or planning. One is called "feasible planning," in which you only design what you feasibly think you can accomplish. Some think that we cannot change the structure of most colleges and universities today because the departmental structure is so embedded that we are not able to change it.

On the other hand, there is another way of looking at the matter. It says, "Maybe not, but why not go through the imaginative exercise of designing a university from the very beginning? It's an exercise those of us who are so intensely interested in college learning can try. Try it out. It won't hurt very much, really. Let your imagination make the picture. You and a group of others now have been selected to design a college from the very beginning. No constraints. It doesn't have to have any departments. It can be anything your imagination wants it to be; anything that you think would be an exciting, valuable learning experience. You can do it while you're driving."

I did it one time. I said, "All right, Churchman, you've been fussing and complaining about this thing you call 'Berkeley,' let's see you design a college. It's up to you to design a college that would appear to you to be a sensible, ideal college." Why would I do that? Because I think if I can do that sometimes, I can see what the blockages are to the ideal.

As I was designing my ideal college, I wanted to say that my new college would have some esoteric learning. I looked in the dictionary and discovered the word "exoteric," which means "knowledge going out to the public." That suggested to me that if I am going to design my ideal, I will tear down the walls of the campus in Berkeley and make the whole city of Berkeley my college.

When you enter my college, you go first to what is called a learning center; but it does not have expert counselors in it. Everybody in the college is contributing their bit to the activities of that center, and the central question of that center is the design of a learning process for each individual. And, though noncommonality resides in the idea that every student is unique, commonality arises in the act of helping individuals design their own learning processes.

How is the ideal college organized? It would work so that everyone shares in trying to help others design their learning process in whatever way they can. Every organization in the city of Berkeley could become a department if it were willing to do so. An office in City Hall, Hink's Department Store, and so on — all could be departments of the university, and one could go there to learn. There might be some esoteric departments (such as mathematics) in their own special buildings where they could feel the kind of isolation they need in their learning process; but, otherwise, students could go out in the city and learn in whatever way they could. The learning center would try to help individuals learn. If some persons need examinations or if they need a degree, both could be obtained at suitable times. Getting a degree raises the question of when the student should leave. When is the university no longer helpful? That is the constant question. Some people in a university system never get the word, "Leave and go out in the world." They are called faculty. This is what my imagination presented me as a gift.

There is a strong pull in all systems design towards conviction about some aspect of the design. Conviction is the enemy of criticism. Criticism says, "I'm not sure this is solid. I'm going to reexamine it." Conviction says, "Dont ask me to reexamine it. I know how it should be."

For example, students need to learn historical facts. At first, that is just a possible design principle; then it becomes a conviction so we have a core course on the history of civilization. Or, as Plato said, students need to learn mathematics, and Plato finally was so convinced of that statement that he put it over the academy: "Let no one enter here without learning mathematics." Or, students need to learn a foreign language so the design says that all students have to do this. No exceptions. You have gone from a possible principle to a conviction. All students need to acquire a certain number of units, or they need to have a common core, and the question is, of course, "How does it help in the design of the student's life to identify, one, ten, or twelve historical episodes?" What has it done to the student? It may have pleased the faculty member who decided to have the student running around trying to find them, but what has it done to the individual student?

To show you how conviction works, here is a story. There was a man who went to a psychiatrist and the psychiatrist sat him down and asked, "What seems to be the trouble?" "Oh, doctor, no real trouble. I just know I'm dead," the man said. The psychiatrist and the patient discussed this for awhile. Then an idea hit the psychiatrist and he said, "Well, put out your little finger." The psychiatrist stuck a pin in it and a glob of blood came out. The psychiatrist said, "See?" And the man said, "Yes, I see." So there it was. Blood was coming out of his finger. The psychiatrist said, "See?" And the patient said, "Sure, I see. Thank God, dead people do bleed."

Mathematical models play an important part in the work of social systems analysts who create integrative models much larger and more complex than my ideal college system. There is a linear programming model, for example, that includes two million variables and 35 thousand constraint equations; it is impossible to deal with without computers. The capability of the computer has gone hand-in-hand with large-scale modeling.

The development of large-scale models was accompanied by a political process in the intellectual community based on the statement, "Models are useful in social systems design." Moving from criticism to conviction, the statement became a principle: "Models are absolutely necessary in social systems design." Thus, we have people in planning who are convinced that there cannot be a good design unless it is based on a large-scale mathematical model.

The political process of moving from criticism to conviction also explains the disciplines. Each of the disciplines is really set up tentatively as an intellectual hypothesis on learning. But what began as a hypothesis has been turned into an absolute conviction, and the way the conviction is expressed is through the word "foundation." Each discipline sees itself as the foundation of all learning. It is a neat trick; a political trick. I mean, I was a logician at one time. Can you have any learning and be illogical? You had better study logic. Can you have any learning and not have a language to express it in? Of course not. You have to express it in a language. Can you have any learning and not have physics? Of course not. Physics is the foundation of all nature. How about psychology? The whole thing is psychology. What is learning except psychology, unless it is sociology?

The disciplines are one of the neatest political maneuvers that have been created in learning in our country. They really put it over on Congress. The biomedical researchers scare the hell out of most congressmen who are in their fifties, by saying, "We've got to develop more knowledge about cancer and respiratory diseases which are the big killers." So the National Institutes of Health get supported. I served three years on the council of one of the NIH institutes, and the whole activity was based on basic research over and over again. Furthermore, they did not get into some of the important infectious diseases, hepatitis, for example, because they had no leads there. The researchers were funded for, what appeared to me to be much irrelevant, research on the basis that if we do not learn more, basically, then we are not going to handle diseases of old age successfully.

One of the neat pieces of politics that we have invented in the professions is what I call "surrogate clients." Who are the clients of a hospital? Common sense replies that the patients or potential patients are the clients. But if you look at the way a hospital is run, that's just not so. Who are the people who are best served in a hospital? If you have ever been in a hospital, you have no question about it. You get a sleeping pill in the evening and you are awakened at five in the morning so that you can be there when the doctor arrives. The idea is, "Serve me well and I'll serve the real client well." But that idea erodes over time, as the surrogate client becomes better served and the real client becomes the victim.

To illustrate this point, I will come back to colleges. I have to admit that I have one of the most beautiful studies at a university campus in the whole San Francisco Bay Area. I have a big library, a telephone, and a secretary. Somehow or other, I do not think the average undergraduate student is as well treated.

Finally, let me say a few words about the interconnectedness of learning itself, specifically of the related workings of reason, politics, and esthetics. Spinoza says there are four levels of education. The lowest level is called hearsay. (The way we normally conduct undergraduate education — I stand up and give a lecture and some students may absorb it and I test what has been absorbed by the midterm or final.) The second level is learned by rule, as we do when we take language courses, or using the 3–4–5 rule in building a roof. The next level is learning the general principles from which the rules follow. That is what we do in physics and chemistry, and, to some extent, in language courses. The highest level Spinoza called intuition. That is when we finally grasp the whole idea. Over the years, I have taught some statistics, and I know what that experience is like. If you teach students statistics in the spring quarter, you will find that the half-life of their knowledge is about three months. It doesn't quite reach the fall quarter. So, when a teacher in the fall quarter says, "Now you are going to use variances and covariances," the student says, "We didn't have those." But knowledge does survive for students who finally see, intuitively, what the whole idea of statistics is. Statistics does have an intuitive base.

At the end of learning, it can be argued, is the beautiful, or I will call it the esthetic, since beautiful has become so overused. Esthetics is the "radiance" of our lives, and that radiance may include the gloomy, sad periods as well as the elated periods. It does not necessarily mean being wildly happy. It simply means that there is a light to human experience. It is true that philosophers have translated esthetics into awful courses that try to distinguish between great art and lesser art. A futile effort, really. Esthetics is something that lives among all of us. To the academic cognitive mind, it is a mystery. For example, as you are driving, having designed your ideal university, try this exercise: Carefully define for me "feeling well." We say, "How are you feeling today?" "Fine." Exactly what do you mean by that response? Give me the dimensions of "feeling well." It is strange that we all pretty much know the difference between feeling well and not feeling well, but it defies our cognitive equipment to say what is the difference. You can say "feeling bad," if you had an ache or a pain, but many people "feel well" with headaches. Pain is not the essence of it. There is something about the nature of your life force that you cannot describe by cognitive means. Define "being conscious." What is that? How do psychologists handle that? They say, "Consciousness is awareness, either of one's self and/or of the outside." Now, you have used another word, awareness, to define consciousness. And where does that get you? And why do you add those two phrases at the end? Only because you could not tell what the word meant in the first place.

Recently, I went to see Yosemite Falls. I would like to tell you precisely what it was like to see Yosemite Falls. But how can I go about describing to you what it meant to see the falls? Trying to do it would ruin the experience unless, perhaps, I broke into music or poetry.

Trying to communicate such a simple, yet awesomely complex, esthetic experience brings me to an often-phrased ideal of learning: not just to learn historical facts or mathematics, but to learn the process of loving to learn. What is it? A measure? What percentage of students in our classes have loved to learn? And to what degree of loving have they come? We cannot measure "loving to learn." It may be that reason and politics themselves come out of the esthetic, just as the ultimate integration of learning resides in the esthetic response. Paul, in Corinthians 13, tried to tell the little religious communities the importance of the esthetic (which he translates as "love") in their lives. I take the liberty of paraphrasing Paul's words as they might be applied to the design of learning: Even though we among us find the perfect design of learning for each individual youth, and even though we designed a perfect implementation of our design, and have not love in the design, it becomes nothing.

*C. West Churchman is professor of Business Administration at
the University of California, Berkeley, and research philosopher at
the Center for Research in Management Science. He is the author,
among many other books, of* The Systems Approach,
Thinking for Decisions, The Design of Inquiring Systems,
and The Systems Approach and Its Enemies.

From "Peter Principle" to interdisciplinary teaching to seminal thinking.

Creative Writing Through Dream Reflection

Richard M. Jones

Should someone, in the foreseeable future, ask me on my death bed if my life had produced any truly original ideas, I would say, yes, one: the one brought to me, almost against my will, by joining the Evergreen faculty. The idea is that Freud's seminal metaphor, the dream censor, from which followed all of his other ideas about the neurotic dimension of the human condition, may be amplified by a companion metaphor, the dream poet, which reveals the equally ubiquitous esthetic dimension of the human condition.

The story of the idea's birth and nurturance is one of irony. Before coming to Evergreen, I held positions at Smith College, Brandeis University, the University of California at Santa Cruz, and Harvard University—covering a period of some fourteen years. During this period, two interests engaged my scholarly activities. One interest sought to enlist modern psychotherapeutic perspectives in the service of enlivening modern educational practices, and produced three books: *An Application of Psychoanalysis to Education* (1960), *Contemporary Educational Psychology* (1967), and *Fantasy and Feeling in Education* (1970a). The other interest, in dreams, led me to develop some expertise as a scientific oneirologist and produced two books: *Ego Synthesis in Dreams* (1962), and *The New Psychology of Dreaming* (1970b).

In 1969, I found myself in the painful grip of the "Peter Principle" in a professorship at Harvard, a position for which I had to thank the writing of the

A. White (Ed.). *New Directions for Teaching and Learning: Interdisciplinary Teaching,* no. 8.
San Francisco: Jossey-Bass, December 1981

books just mentioned. However, the position turned out to be one in which I could do nothing that was relevant to the further pursuit of either interest: dreaming about teaching or teaching about dreaming. An opportunity came along to help plan, then to teach in the Evergreen State College, and I took it. The college that we planned, now in its eighth controversially successful year, has no departments, requirements, majors, courses, or grades. Instead, groups of students and small teams of faculty contract to work together full time (for a semester, a year, or two years) to study a theme, solve a problem, or complete a project of interdisciplinary scope. When we finish such a project, we write to each other, as candidly as possible, about the influences we had on each other in the process. Considerations of *what* is learned are secondary to considerations of *how* to learn. There can be no competing commitments for either students or faculty. Whatever it takes to get the job done well and satisfactorily — skills to be learned, information to be acquired, research to be done — cannot be arbitrarily obstructed. There is no place to hide, almost anything can be tried, and the system of evaluation by mutual reflection tends to keep most of us honest.

During my first year at Evergreen I was asked by a former student (Arthur Warmoth, by that time a prominent figure in the Association for Humanistic Psychology), who was composing a textbook on humanistic psychology, to write the chapter on dreams. It appeared to be an easy task, involving only a slight rewriting of a chapter I had already written on contemporary approaches to dream interpretation, so I agreed. But when it came time to meet the agreement, it dawned on me that I had, for some time, tended to reflect on my own dreams in ways that none of these analytical methods sought explicitly to do. I realized I had become unable to be content with merely understanding them; for optimal fulfillment had come to reside in the enjoyment of them, as one might enjoy a piece of music or a beautiful building. Sometimes the enjoyment followed the understanding; sometimes it superseded understanding. Not that I was ungrateful for the deepened sense of self-awareness that analyzing my dreams gave me; rather, I had come to take the various interpretations and their consequent illuminations of my personal self for granted. I had become truly less interested in what my dreams could say to me and more interested in what I, as their author, could say to them. So I determined to write the chapter on the entertainment of dreams.

About this time, while I was learning as an Evergreen faculty member to lead seminars in biology, anthropology, philosophy, and literature, in addition to those in psychology, the students asked one day if I had been an expert in anything before coming to Evergreen. Yes, I replied, I had been something of an expert in dream psychology. Would I give them an extra workshop in that? Thus was begun the dream reflection seminar. In its initial form it merely involved an hour and a half a week during which I attempted to teach the students not only how to understand their dreams but how to enjoy them, as I had learned to enjoy my own. Of course, the prospect of gathering addi-

tional data for the chapter was welcome, but was a very subsidiary consideration. In truth, I perceived the writing of the chapter as a kind of last hurrah in
my career as a scholar. I thought well of the books I had written, but an important aspect of my decision to move to Evergreen was the opportunity to devote
all of my interests and energies to teaching, and none of them to research and
publication. In 1971 I had no idea that another book was hatching — much less
that it would be my most valuable one.

The dream reflection seminar was a popular success and in the following four years it evolved into this more elaborate format:

1. First we read a work of literature and discuss it in a seminar, from
the points of view of the possible meanings intended by the author, the meanings suggested by the text, and our personal responses to the work.

2. On a subsequent morning, someone brings to the seminar a dream
and his or her written reflections on it — typed and dittoed, so that everyone
has a copy.

3. The dreamer reads the dream and the reflections.

4. As we close our eyes and try to visualize our own versions of the
dream's imagery, the dreamer reads the dream again. This has the effect of
calming inevitable personal jitters and getting us into a studious frame of
mind.

5. For approximately the next two hours, we discuss the dream from
two points of view: What it may be saying to us and what we may be prompted
to say back to it. Thus, our objectives are to understand the dream *and* to
enjoy it. In this latter venture we learn to respond to the dream's play on words
and images; its sound symbolisms and flourishes of synesthesia; its visually
alliterative sequences; its deployments of the figurative and literal; its double
entendres, stagings, artifices, puns, and jokes. The discussion is guided by the
rule that we are free to advance any hunch, speculation, or intuition; ask any
question; or offer any interpretation or outright guess that may help us to
achieve the two objectives: understanding and enjoyment. This freedom is
limited only by the common acknowledgment that the dreamer will be the ultimate judge of the correctness of the understanding and of the tastefulness of
the enjoyment.

6. Then we go off individually and write for two hours. The dreamer's
writing usually consists of summarizing the highlights of the discussion and
extending his reflections on the dream. The rest of us write something — a
poem, an essay, a letter, a story, some dialogue — that links our reflections on
the dream to our understanding of the week's common reading assignment.
This is the most challenging step in the sequence, and, when successful, the
most rewarding.

7. Then we reconvene as a seminar, and read what we wrote to each
other. The writings tend to be of such startlingly liberated quality as to generate a mood of uncommon mutual respect — sometimes falling not far short of
shock. Here are some samples:

Counter Feat

The computer
Escalates
Picking its mountains
Out of Helen's teeth
While the goy on the bicycle
Incestuously
With rings on his fingers and clubs on his heels
Writes up four dollar bills
On ancient plates
Carved out of looted slabs
Which the Byronic hero
Interpreted as sexual allegories
(At hyperbole velocities)
To initiate schizoid fission
In the fourfold genetic temple
Where the hermaphroditic Athena
Protects the spiral strands
Of the terminal memory bank
From serpent spirochetes
And Aurora unfolds her mushroom chandelier
In the pentalic temple
Signaling to the Parthian cock
That Atlantic is within

And when evening sets on the fever
Of the earth-exiled poet
The temple of the virgin
Will become an open vehicle
(Mistress to an apocalypse)
The brother of the Rebel
Shall sign for the Tao
And the guilty lame duck diplomat
Shall become bicycling infinity
Till his keys are tangled in the red tape
Of immaculate calculation

        Edward Ketcham

(The reading was William Blake's *The Mental Traveler*.)

I would like to live in a circle
become androgynous
walk in an alley
between brick buildings

both hands occupied
and both of those hands
occupied
looking in all directions
simultaneously
comprehending
roundness.
                Steven Weinberg
(The reading was Robert Frost's *The Road Not Taken*.)

8. Then the writings are typed and printed. Each week, everyone receives copies of the previous week's writings.

The tone of the seminar tends to be one of scholarly good humor. Therapeutic gains in self-knowledge are expected and accepted, but the prevailing expectation is that personal insights will be extended to grace some aspect of our academic commitments with personal meaning. Here is the way one student, Lloyd Houston, described the experience:

We come in alone and we go out alone, but in between we have each other; the tight throats, the full and empty days, the tears, the unions of minds and hearts, the laughter, the limbo of chaos—the magic. Feeling the moment as it breaks on the nerve of the heart, turns time timeless, as here and now cease to matter and we grope for the mysteries— the magic. Of sharing and knowing, and sharing the knowing and knowing the sharing.

Hear a quiet woman talk of her life and feel the thread that binds her to me, as though we'd loved. Hear a tender man who turns his dreams— and mine—into wriggling, flashing poetry. To find a watch pocket we thought the world had taken from us, or a blue tin cup we thought our childhood had lost, or a new blue streetcar named desire, or a hidden hinge hitched to integrity, or the real thing in a coke bottle. . .

All of us have been burned. We have a common past but it gives us no cohesion. Each alone. No village anymore. No more we . . . only the slide toward un-we.

No mythology sought in unison. No common bond with the strength of history in it. Forced, all of us, in this way or that, to create our mythologies from personal experience, lived or dreamed; having, like it or not, ready or not, to make heroes of ourselves.

"You, whoever you are," is probably the most repeated phrase in *Leaves of Grass*. Whitman saw us coming. No, he was already one of us. Is there an "other" to whom the modern poet can speak? Is there no "other" — no beloved, no audience, no God — what is the point, the possibility even, of turning private vision into public song?

The uncertainty is still there within each of us, every Friday. But rather than holding us back, spontaneity stifled, we become instead almost child-like in freedom and vitality of mind. And then the afternoon writing shows that we are anything but children. The quality of uncertainty characteristic of the dream reflection seminar seems to act as a catalyst freeing our thoughts from their usual musty pathways. The integrity and quality of "the play" becomes the prevailing concern. Everyone becomes more sensitive to everyone, more civil, more thoughtful, more human. And, as is true of a good play, the sign of a good dream reflection seminar is always lots of hearty laughter.

By this time, the dream reflection-creative writing seminar sequence was becoming an Evergreen tradition, having been taken up and adapted to their own teaching styles by more than a dozen colleagues. (Leo Daugherty, David Hitchens, Will Humphreys, Mark Levensky, Earle McNeil, Tom Maddox, Charles Pailthorp, Peter Sinclair, Bob Sluss, David Marr, Diana Cushing, Don Finkel, Wendy Schofield, and Edward McQuarrie.)

Following a particularly dramatic seminar that had been led jointly by Pete Sinclair and me, the dream poet suggested itself as a metaphor for the set of attitudes and expectations that distinguished dream reflection from dream interpretation, and I later found myself summarizing another chapter as follows:

Recall that Freud's theory of dreams was centered on a metaphor drawn from an analogy: The metaphor of the dream censor drawn from a perception of dreams as analogous to neurotic symptoms. This choice of metaphor predetermined the parameters of the theory: preoccupation with the disguised causes of the dream; a predilection to conceive the transformative processes of dream formation as work; the attributing of greater importance to what can be deduced from the associations to a dream than to the dream itself; the investing of authority as to questions of relevance in the objectivity of the analyst; and the assumption that dream interpretation must be a comparatively private enterprise, a confidential dialogue between a patient and his analyst.

As we have sought over the past five years to involve dreams in the educational process, we have been guided by a companion metaphor, that of the dream poet. As the dream censor is drawn from a perception of dreams as analogous to neurotic systems, the dream poet is drawn from a perception of dreams as analogous to artistic visions. As the dream censor invites preoccupation with the disguised causes of a dream, the dream poet courts the liberating effects of dreams. As the dream censor invites the view of the transformative processes of dream formation as one of work, the dream poet invites the view of the same processes as one of play. As the dream censor requires that we place the locus of authority as to questions of relevance in the objectivity of the analyst, the dream poet requires that we place this locus in the subjectivity of the dreamer. And, as the dream censor insists that dream interpretation be a private enterprise, the dream poet requires that dream reflection be a public, collective enterprise.

Meanwhile, the process of collegial influence proved to be anything but one-way. As new colleagues expressed an interest in the educational technique, I had, perforce, to learn something of their universe of discourse, so as to make sense of my metaphor. In time, I had to provide the dream poet with credentials from the points of view of Alexander Marshack, Lancelot Law Whyte, Michael Polanyi, Norman O. Brown, Herbert Marcuse, Morse Peckham, Jean Piaget, Susanne Langer, and Lewis Mumford—among others. For example, I have been led to speculate that the reclamation process described earlier by my former student, Lloyd Houston, may find its parallel at the level of cultural evolution. In this I follow Michael Polanyi's envisonment of the postscientific age into which he thinks we may be moving. An age in which our current addiction to articulate knowledge and literal meaning may become moderated under the influence of rediscovering the values of tacit knowledge and figurative meaning. An age in which, while we continue to play the doubting game, we shall increasingly permit ourselves to also play the believing game. As I read Polanyi, the development of science, with its subjugation of tacit knowledge to articulate knowledge, was a necessary and valuable liberating influence, against the bondage to which the capacity for belief had become tied to theocratic dogmas. But, as I read him further, this revolutionary achievement of science has now occurred and is irreversible and safely established as one of the basic precepts of human consciousness. The further development of historical consciousness may lie in the taking for granted of this achievement, and of restoring to our capacity for doubtless knowing our capacity for truly believing in what we know. Efforts to reemphasize the primary processes of metaphorical meaning can only serve, now, to revolutionize this achievement of science, not by substituting subjective belief for objective knowledge, which science has made impossible, but by investing the acquisition of objective knowledge with intellectual passion and qualities of personal conviction that, as contemporary students and teachers well know, the acquisition of knowledge can lack.

As a sabbatical leave approached, there was nothing to do but write another book: *The Dream Poet* (Schenkman, 1980). The book describes a proven new approach to the teaching of creative writing, and goes on to establish the dream poet as perhaps as seminal a metaphor in exploring the esthetic dimension of the human condition as was Freud's dream censor in exploring the neurotic dimension of the human condition — ending on a note of speculation, similar to those sounded by Langer and Mumford, that rapid eye movement (dreaming) sleep may have been a key item in the constellation of factors involved in the evolution of speech.

So much for my resolution to do nothing but teach! Had I stayed at Harvard, I would have written at least one other book. I would have had to; but it could not have been as rich as this one. This book's conception was due to the confluence of three quite specific conditions: (1) My prior knowledge of the subject, (2) Evergreen teaching conditions (especially the mutual full-time component), and (3) the opportunity of having to amplify my prior knowledge of the subject by way of working intimately with knowledgeable colleagues from many other disciplines.

References

Jones, R. M. *An Application of Psychoanalysis to Education.* Springfield, Ill.: Thomas, 1960.
Jones, R. M. *Ego Synthesis in Dreams.* Cambridge, Mass.: Schenkman, 1962.
Jones, R. M. *Contemporary Educational Psychology.* New York: Harper & Row, 1967.
Jones, R. M. *Fantasy and Feeling in Education.* New York: Harper & Row, 1970a.
Jones, R. M. *The New Psychology of Dreaming.* New York: Viking, 1970b.
Jones, R. M. *The Dream Poet.* Cambridge, Mass.: Schenkman, 1980.

Prior to joining the planning faculty of the Evergreen State College, Richard Jones taught at Brandeis University, the University of California at Santa Cruz, and Harvard University.

*The Harvard house system provided the means for developing a
cross-disciplinary course dealing with political, art, music, dance,
and literary history in late medieval Burgundy.*

Burgundy:
The Rise and Fall
of the Middle Realm

Arthur L. Loeb

This is an account of the events leading up to the creation of a nondepartmen-
tal credit course at Harvard, entitled "Burgundy: The Rise and Fall of the
Middle Realm," and a report on that course as it was given in the spring of
1979. Because I possess none of the departmental qualifications to teach such a
course, Harvard's tolerance in permitting this experiment will be understand-
able only when certain autobiographical data are presented. Next, a brief
history of the Burgundian realm, roughly between 1350 and 1530, will clarify
why this particular region and era are particularly attractive for a cross-disci-
pinary course. Finally, there is an account of the course itself, its various an-
cillary events, and a sampling of the projects completed by the students in partial fulfillment of the course requirements.

It was as a musician that I became involved in the Cambridge Drama
Festival of 1956. Two of the plays in which I participated that summer were
Shakespeare's *Henry V* and Shaw's *Saint Joan*. After officiating at the coronation
of Charles VII in Rheims and narrowly escaping injury in the Battle of Agincourt, I began to wonder about the relation between the events depicted in the
two plays. Since I was at that time on the faculty of the Electrical Engineering
Department at M.I.T., the answer was neither at my fingertips nor on my

A. White (Ed.). *New Directions for Teaching and Learning: Interdisciplinary Teaching,* no. 8.
San Francisco: Jossey-Bass, December 1981

bookshelves. Perhaps I, as a musician, would have returned to my *Dufay* or *Josquin*, and, as solid-state scientist, might have put the summer's activities behind me as a pleasant experience. However, I, as a structurist, was obsessed with the meaningful relationship between two things.

Subsequently, I performed dances from a dance manual owned by the Burgundian princess, Margaret of Austria, and participated in observances commemorating the anniversary of the death of Burgundian composer Josquin des Pres. These varied experiences ultimately led to the proposal of a credit course, "Burgundy: the Rise and Fall of the Middle Realm," at Harvard. The purpose of such a course was to show that the works of art and of the mind that are studied in disciplines known as musicology, art history, theology, and history of science are, in fact, related to each other and to the important events of the time in which they were created, and can be understood and appreciated better when studied in unified context. This course was offered under the auspices of the Committee on New Departmental Instruction, which approves and supervises courses when the scope of the course exceeds or does not fall within either the core curriculum or the domain of a particular department. Such courses are usually presented within one of the undergraduate Harvard houses, with which the instructor is associated, although the enrollment is not limited to members of the sponsoring house.

Organization of the Course

To teach a course of this nature in sufficient depth requires the assistance of a number of experts in art history, literature, music, and dance as well as political, architectural, and religious history. Here lies one of the strengths of the Harvard house system: A cross section of the traditional academic departments in reasonably intimate association in one of the thirteen undergraduate houses. The active support of the masters and a large number of members of the Senior Common Room of Dudley House made this possible.

The method of teaching was that used in the Department of Visual and Environmental Studies, namely, of learning by personal experience. Although it is difficult to give students a first-hand experience of living in the fourteenth and fifteenth centuries, the re-creation of a Burgundian banquet as an all-Dudley House event provided a focus for many of the students' term projects. For example, paintings and miniatures were studied for the information they provided: The musical instruments in Jan van Eyck's *Ghent Altarpiece* were compared with the instruments used in a performance of Dufay's *Missa Se la face ay pale*. To design the space needed for some of the court dances, miniatures were studied. As linear perspective was only just coming into its own, questions about the representation of space and distance arose, and the number of place settings and other objects served as clues. Costumes for dancers, musicians, and other courtiers were designed by studying paintings and tapestries; correlations were found between the dance movements and the length of the ladies' trains in different regions and periods. The English victories at Crécy, Poitiers, and Agincourt led to a study of the crossbow and an attempt at a reconstruction. The Angevin/Burgundian art of heraldry provided the banners for the banquet hall as well as a very fine paper on the graphic representation of dynastic relations on coats of arms.

Planning the banquet menu brought up questions about the availability of spices, their uses in medicine, the strategic control of the spice trade routes, and the economy in general. Burgundian wine was already an important item of trade in the Middle Ages, and the optimal conditions of soil and climate as well as trade routes provided topics for two of the term projects.

There was no final examination in the course. Requirements were a brief verbal progress report at midterm, a final report during reading period on the term project, and a final written report. The term projects, in addition to these written reports, included a number of concrete illustrations made according to medieval prescription including a meat pie, a marzipan gryphon, banners, mentioned earlier, a gilded nef, a chanson composed to a text by Charles d'Orleans, the performance of three Burgundian court dances, and a sample of tapestry showing the Golden Fleece, woven according to the method of Arras. These offerings were presented and displayed at the banquet, as was the custom of the fifteenth century.

One-third of the students in the course were members of Dudley House. Seven members of the Dudley House Senior Common Room actively participated in the course, making this a true house activity.

The enrollment of twenty-seven undergraduates, one law school student, and four auditors was much higher than had been expected. To somewhat maintain the seminar character, the class was divided into six task forces: Food and Viticulture, History and Religion, Iconography, Women's Biographies, Music, and Dance.

The class met jointly for three hours per week; in addition, each task force met at regularly scheduled intervals, for example, the Music and Dance task forces met for two hours each week.

A Brief Glance at the History of Burgundy

Though other historical periods and cultures could have served as a focus for this kind of course, the Burgundian realm, at its height and during its early decline, proved particularly suitable. The Burgundians originated on the island of Bornholm in the Baltic Sea. In the early fourth century they lived in the Rhine valley. The middle-high German *Song of Nibelungen*, written around 1200, tells of their King Gunther, his sister Kriemhild's marriage to the Netherlandish hero Sigfrid, and the war between the Huns and the Burgundians. The latter were defeated and settled in southeastern France where they allied themselves with the Franks. When heirs of Charlemagne divided the Frankish empire into three parts, Burgundy became part of the middle realm;

but when the middle portion was in turn split between west and east, the Duchy of Burgundy was incorporated into France, whereas the County of Burgundy (Franche Comté) lay within the boundary of the Holy Roman Empire (Germany).

The period 1350-1530, which we now tend to perceive as a transition from the Middle Ages to the Renaissance, was a period of formation of the modern European states. The Burgundian domains, with their brilliant courts, intense artistic and musical development, and individual style, represented a culture neither French nor German, following and in turn influencing developments in Renaissance Italy. This period and geographical region are very appropriate for teaching the connections between what have become the traditional academic disciplines, as exemplified by the influence of English composers on those of the Low Countries; the patronage of the van Eycks and the Limburg brothers by the dukes of Burgundy and Berry; the poetry of Christine de Pisan and her views on the Burgundian-Armagnac Civil war; and the influences of Jan Hus and the Modern Devotion on the Reformation.

Progress of the Course

After an introductory organizational meeting, Ann Fehn from the Department of Germanic Languages and Literature lectured on the mythological prehistory of the Burgundians as described in the *Song of the Nibelungen.* The historiographic aspect of Fehn's lecture was important: different periods look differently at their past. The middle German poem was compared with Wagner's nineteenth-century operatic cycle. The nineteenth-century revival of interest in the Middle Ages was further illustrated in a recital by David Beyer and myself of Johannes Brahms's "Romances" from Tieck's *Magellone.* Tieck was one of the prime movers in the medieval revival, and his *Magellone* describes the early connections between the Kingdom of Naples and that part of the ancient Burgundian Kingdom known as Provence.

During the remainder of February, I covered the history of fourteenth-century Burgundy and the Low Countries, commencing with the Battle of the Golden Spurs in 1302, in which the Flemish defeated the French, and the beginning of the Hundred Years' War. The capture of King Jean II of France and his youngest son Philippe by the English at Poitiers in 1356, and the death of blind King Jan of Bohemia at Crécy in 1346 were focal events; the former because Philippe's fierce loyalty to his father earned him the Duchy of Burgundy as well as the title "le Hardi," while King Jan was not only father to Emperor Charles IV and to Bona, wife of King Jean II of France, but also the patron to Guillaume Machaut, eminent poet, composer, and diplomat.

The marriage of Philippe Le Hardi to Marguerite, heiress to the counties of Burgundy, Artois, Flanders, and the Duchy of Brabant linked the Duchy of Burgundy to the Low Countries during the final quarter of the fourteenth century. The emergence of Burgundy as a political power, together with the intermittent insanity of the French King Charles VI, led to a civil war between adherents of the Burgundian and Orleans branches of the Valois family.

At this point in the course, Robert Bousquet, Department of Romance Languages, University of Lowell, delivered a guest lecture about Charles d'Orleans as a literary figure and the *formes fixes* (rondeau, ballade, and virelay). Bosquet gave us some beautiful readings of Charles d'Orlean's French and English poems.

During March, Marianne Teuber, art historian, lectured on the van Eycks, van der Weyden, and the miniaturists. The historical survey proceeded to the Treaty of Arras in 1435, including important related events in England such as the reigns of Richard II and Henry IV, the Battle of Agincourt, the manifold dynastic marriages, the assassinations of the Dukes of Orleans and Burgundy, the connections of Jeanne d'Arc to the House of Orleans, and the long literary career of Christine de Pisan, starting with her service to the Burgundian Court and culminating in her eulogoy of Jeanne d'Arc. Then, Ingrid Brainard, a musicologist and dance historian, delivered a guest lecture on Burgundian Court Dance and conducted a workshop to teach some of the dances to the entire class. The members of the task force on Dance also took Brainard's course on Court Dance offered under the auspices of the Harvard-Radcliffe Office of the Arts.

Jean Doten from the Department of Music lectured on performance practice and the style characteristic of Burgundian music, with particular reference to the *Missa Se la face ay pale* of Guillaume Dufay. This mass was performed by the Collegium Iosquinum under the direction of myself at the Busch-Reisinger Museum.

Midterm reports and the spring recess accounted for the remainder of March, after which Ian Siggins of the Divinity School lectured on the Modern Devotion and related developments in religion in the Low Countries. The historical survey resumed with the Treaty of Arras, covering the loosening of the Anglo-Burgundian alliance, the estrangement of Charles VII and his son Louis, who sought refuge at the Burgundian Court, and in turn, the estrangement between Duke Philippe Le Bon of Burgundy and his son Charles Le Téméraire. The rivalry between Louis XI and Charles Le Téméraire, the battle of Nancy, and the civil war between York and Lancaster led to the final period in Burgundian history, that of Marie of Burgundy and her husband Maximilian of Habsburg, and their children Philip the Fair and Marguerite. As Gabrielle Lemlich remarked in her brilliant term paper, Burgundian history could be considered ended by 1530, when the peace between the two erstwhile sisters-in-law Louise de Savoye (mother of King François I of France) and Marguerite (aunt of Emperor Charles V) permanently returned the Duchy of Burgundy proper to France, but permanently separated Flanders from France as well.

During April, we were honored to have Kenneth Conant of the

Department of Fine Arts lecture on Cluny and early Burgundian monastic architecture. Konrad Oberhuber also from the Department of Fine Arts spoke about art at the court of Maximilian, and Franklin Ford of the Department of History rounded off the course with a lecture on the heritage of the continuing influence of Burgundy through later centuries.

On April 27, the course concluded with a symposium, comprised of lectures by the guest lecturers in the course as well as by other specialists. This symposium established a real sense of community between the participating scholars and raised the hope for periodic meetings of this kind. The lectures were as follows:

> Ingrid Brainard: "An Exotic Court Dance and Dance Spectacle
> of the Renaissance: La Moresca."
> Ian Siggins: "The Preaching of a Disciple: The Sermon Books of
> Johannes Herolt, O.P."
> Arthur L. Loeb: "Kinship Graphs"
> Peter Jordan: "Brittany"
> Robert Bousquet: "The Sorrows of Marguerite of Austria,
> as Reflected in the Music of Pierre de la Rue"
> Konrad Oberhuber: "Is There a Middle Style of Painting?"
> Geoffrey Hindley: "Low Countries' Influence on English Composers
> in the Early Fifteenth Century"
> Barbara K. Wheaton: "The Medieval Banquet: What It Is
> and How To Eat It"

The final lecture was followed appropriately by the banquet, for which Wheaton acted as a very patient, knowledgeable, and amiable consultant and at which she presented her cooked peacock in full-feathered splendor.

The Term Projects

At Harvard, the period between the end of classes and the beginning of examinations, lasting approximately two weeks, is known as the Reading Period. Some courses continue during this period, while others suspend class meetings. In this course, this period was used to permit each student to present a brief report to the class and to incorporate feedback from faculty and students into the final term paper, which was due at the end of the Reading Period.

A sampling of the titles of the term projects gives an idea of the range of interests and study provoked by the course: "Erasmus and the Mystic Tradition," "The Role of Women in Courtly Life and Love," "Medieval Medicine in France and Italy," "Wine in Burgundy," "Mythical Beasts in the Middle Ages," "Manuscript Books in Burgundy from the Middle Ages to the Renaissance," "Behind the Arras: the Tradition of Weaving in Burgundy,"

"Burgundian Court Dance," "The Impact of the Establishment of the New Middle Kingdom: the Burgundian Possessions in the Low Countries," and "Protocol and Courtly Etiquette."

Arthur L. Loeb received his Ph.D. degree in chemical physics from Harvard where he presently teaches design science. A musician and visual artist, his books include Color and Symmetry *(John Wiley) and* Space Structures, Their Harmony and Counterpoint *(Addison-Wesley). He has contributed to* R. Buckminster Fuller's Synergetics *and to texts on wave mechanics and colloid science.*

Astronomical or astrological knowledge enables scholars to decode scientific or metaphorical allusions in the poetry of Chaucer, Skelton, and Donne and sometimes to date the composition of the works.

Transdisciplinary Intersections: Astronomy and Three Early English Poets

Owen Gingerich

One of the most enjoyable books that I have read outside of my scientific discipline is Richard D. Altick's *The Scholar Adventurers* (1960). His stories of the forger unmasked by literary detection or Pepys's shorthand cracked by cryptographers appeal to my own sense of historical sleuthing and of the scholar as hero.

In particular, I am fascinated by Altick's retelling of how the composition of Chaucer's *Troilus and Criseyde* was dated. In this charming tale, the pleasantly scheming Pandarus has succeeded at last in bringing under the same roof the valiant warrior, Troilus, and the lady for whose love he has been languishing, the lovely young widow Criseyde. Having hidden Troilus in a closet, Pandarus entertains his unsuspecting niece at supper. By and by she takes her leave, but Pandarus looks out the window, and "all was on a flood."

> The bent moon with her pale horns,
> Saturn, and Jove in Cancer joined were
> That such a rain from heaven poured down
> That every man and woman that was there
> Had of that smoky rain a full real fear.
> (III. 624–8)

A. White (Ed.). *New Directions for Teaching and Learning: Interdisciplinary Teaching*, no. 8. San Francisco: Jossey-Bass, December 1981

Criseyde, being a sensible as well as a splendidly beautiful young woman, agrees that it would be folly indeed to venture out on such a night. So Pandarus escorts her to his best bedroom, bids her good night, and hastens back to the closet where Troilus has been garreted.

But instead of spoiling a good story, let us follow Altick as he shifts the scene to the 1920s, over five centuries after Chaucer created his pioneering novel. Princeton's Robert K. Root, a distinguished Chaucer specialist, was pondering the text of *Troilus and Criseyde*. Scholars had been able to agree only that this masterpiece had been written sometime between 1373 and 1386. Was it possible that Chaucer had joined the moon with Saturn and Jupiter in the constellation Cancer because they actually *were* there at the time he wrote?

Perplexed, Root took his problem to Henry Norris Russell at Princeton Observatory. Excited by this prospect of an interdisciplinary collaboration, Russell agreed to investigate, and he quickly rediscovered what many astronomers before him, including Kepler, had known.

Each time Jupiter overtakes Saturn in the sky, it is approximately 120° farther west along the ecliptic, that is, four signs backward along the zodiac. Thus, if Jupiter and Saturn meet in Cancer, three conjunctions or sixty years later will find them once again in the same sign. However, the 120° is only approximate—actually the figure is closer to 117°. If a conjunction occurs near the beginning of Cancer, then 60 years later another conjunction will occur 9° farther into the sign of Cancer, and so on until the pattern moves into the next sign. In other words, the conjunctions will occur in Cancer every 60 years for approximately 200 years, to be followed by a period of over 600 years in which the two planets *never* meet in Cancer.

Russell's calculations showed that Saturn and Jupiter came into conjunction in the Spring of 1385 on the boundary of Gemini and Cancer and by the middle of May the planets had moved into Cancer and were joined by the lunar crescent—"the bent moon with her pale horns." Such an omen—the rare pairing of the two slowest moving planets and in a "watery" sign—could hardly have been overlooked by Chaucer and his contemporaries. Assured of the year and season for which Chaucer conceived his storm scene, Root examined the voluminous chronicle of English history compiled by the fourteenth-century monk Thomas Walsingham, and there, under 1385, he found a reference to a celestial conjunction and to the foreboding that it aroused in the English citizenry. Then, as Walsingham recounts, in the afternoon of July 14, 1385, a terrific thunderstorm broke over England, the like of which had not been seen by mortal men. With a deft artistic hand Chaucer had merged the two separate events—the unusual planetary conjunction and the great storm—into one. Thus, with their scientific-literary collaboration, Root and Russell had established that *Troilus and Criseyde* could not have been written earlier than the summer of 1385.

I am sure that Chaucer's appeal for me lies at least partly in the English poet's own deep concern with astronomy. *Canterbury Tales,* like *Troilus and Cri-*

seyde, includes frequent lines bearing witness to the lure that astronomy held for the poet. A particularly famous astronomical allusion occurs within a few first lines of its prologue: "and the young sun hath in the Ram his half-course run." To those familiar with the sun's annual motion around the ecliptic, the meaning is clear: The sun is halfway through the constellation Aries, so that the pilgrimage was beginning two weeks after the vernal equinox, early in April.

Chaucer's interest in astronomy stretched beyond the scattered references in his poetical works. It is well known that he wrote a detailed *Treatise on the Astrolabe*. Like much of the material in his poetry, the treatise was freely translated from other sources, but this does not detract from the fact that he was interested enough to prepare the material systematically for his ten-year-old son, "Litel Lowys." Not only did he write out the instructions for making and using this astronomical instrument, but he promised a further section on another, more complicated, device for finding "the moving of the celestial bodies."

This subsequent treatise long remained unknown; then about twenty-five years ago, a historian of science, Derek J. de Solla Price, stumbled across an anonymous manuscript in the Peterhouse Library in Cambridge, England, a manuscript in Middle English closely fitting the description of the promised Chaucerian text. Price edited the manuscript as *The Equatorie of the Planetis* (1969), making an excellent case that this was not only the missing work, but a manuscript in Chaucer's own hand.

On several occasions in his writings Chaucer uses the positions of the planets, as might be found from his equatorium, to set up horoscopic configurations that explain some fatalistic twist of plot. One such appears in the *Man of Law's Tale*. Constance, a devout Christian, is compelled to marry a pagan sultan; the poet, wishing to set the stage for the ensuing misfortunes, cries forth in an apostrophe:

> O first moving! Cruel firmament
> That crowds with thy diurnal sway
> And hurls all from east to west
> That naturally would hold another way.
> Thy crowding set the heavens in such array
> At the beginning of this first voyage,
> That cruel Mars hath slain this marriage.
>
> Unfortunate tortuous ascendant,
> Of which the Lord is fallen helpless, alas!
> Out of his angle into the darkest house.
> O Mars O Atazir, as in this case!
> O feeble moon, unhappy is thy pace!
> Knit to where thou art not well received,
> Thrust from thy place, thy powers waived. (295–308)

When I first began looking at Chaucer's astronomy, I found Walter Clyde Curry's *Chaucer and the Medieval Sciences* (1960) a particularly helpful book. He provides an intricate analysis of Constance's horoscope, taking cognizance of the several technical astrological expressions: tortuous, ascendant, Lord, angle, house, and atazir. For example, Mars is the "Lord" of the zodiacal signs Aries and Scorpio, and these signs are Mars's "domicile." The "tortuous" signs are Aries, Taurus, Gemini, Capricorn, Aquarius, and Pisces. The sky at a given moment is divided into twelve "houses," not be confused with the twelve zodiacal signs; the "ascendant" is the house containing the part of the sky about to rise in the east. The ascendant is one of four symmetrically placed houses called the "angles." Each of the twelve houses is associated with certain events or factors in a typical lifetime, and the "darkest house," representing death or captivity, is the zone immediately above the eastern horizon.

Curry reconstructs an elaborate celestial configuration, placing Mars in conjunction with a crescent moon in the constellation Libra. Then, according to his interpretation, the moon and Mars move by their slow monthly or annual motions into the sign of Scorpio, the "darker" of the two domiciles of Mars. It was many years after I first read Curry's book that I realized that his explanation not only completely missed the phrases "O first moving!" and "diurnal sway" but misinterpreted "the darkest house" as well. Mars, rather than lying in Libra, must be in its tortuous domicile, Aries, poised in the ascendant ready to advance out of its angle into the dark house of death and captivity. This occurs naturally through the daily rotation of the heavens, that is, the "first moving." I was about to rush my alternative interpretation into print when I discovered that this criticism had long since been noted by John Matthews Manly (see Robinson, 1957) and more recently by John North (1969).

Dating Skelton's *Garland of Laurel*

My own adventure in astronomy-poetry intersection came about in 1962 when Melvin J. Tucker, then an instructor at M.I.T., brought an intriguing problem to my attention. He had been inspecting the *Garland of Laurel*, an allegorical poem by Tudor poet John Skelton. The poem takes for its scene the floral garland awarded to the poet laureate, and includes a lengthy poetic accolade to a bevy of ladies of the court, whose identities challenge any Skelton analyst. Tucker reported that identifications could be more easily made with people in the 1490s than in the 1520s when the poem was published.

Skelton opened the *Garland of Laurel* with seven remarkably astronomical lines:

> Erecting my sight toward the zodiac
> The signs XII for to behold afar,

> When Mars retrogradant reversed his back,
>   Lord of the year in his orbicular,
> Put up his sword, for he could make no war,
>   And when Lucina plenarly did shine,
> Scorpion ascending degrees twice nine . . .

After showing me the opening lines, Tucker posed a challenging question: Had the Tudor poet described an actual astronomical configuration, and would it shed any light on the date of composition of the poem? The answer could contain significant ramifications for Skeltonian scholarship, since the *Garland of Laurel* presented a peculiar poem in the poet's literary development. Published in 1523 and dedicated to his former antagonist Cardinal Wolsey, the allegorical dream form of the poem shows a close literary kinship to Skelton's earlier work, but it stood in marked contrast to a series of political satires and a recent vicious attack on Wolsey himself. Tucker had already noted that at the end of 1522 Skelton's chief protector at court had retired, leaving the poet vulnerable to Wolsey's displeasure. Had Skelton dusted off an earlier poem to demonstrate his reform?

Earlier critics had, of course, noticed the reference to the retrogression of Mars in the third line, but since this phenomenon occurs approximately every two years, the retrogression did not pose any serious constraint in choosing a date for the poem, with 1523 being the popular choice. Nevertheless, the stanza contains an unusually precise numerical datum neglected by earlier critics: "Scorpion ascending degrees twice nine." Also, besides the two other pieces of astronomical information (that Mars is retrograding and that the moon is full), the opening lines contain two potentially useful astrological phrases: "Lord of the year" and "Put up his sword, for he could make no war."

Since the ascendant is the part of the sky just about to rise over the eastern horizon, the phrase "Scorpion ascending degrees twice nine" suggested that Scorpio 18° would be on the eastern horizon. Mars retrogrades for the several weeks when it is opposite the sun, and of course a full moon is opposite the sun. Hence Mars and the moon must have been in conjunction — but does Skelton's stanza also imply that they were located at Scorpio 18°?

At the time when Tucker introduced me to the *Garland of Laurel* horoscope, I was in the process of computing a 4,500-year planetary ephemeris, which was to be published as the Stahlman/Gingerich *Solar and Planetary Longitudes*. With these tables, I found that Mars would have retrograded in Scorpio in April and May of the years 1463, 1495, 1510, and 1542. In particular, on May 8, 1495 we found that the full moon would have risen at sunset in close conjunction with a brilliant first-magnitude Mars near Scorpio 18°. Tucker and I were delighted at this turn of events because such a remarkable configuration could scarcely have been anticipated at the start of our investigation. Furthermore, the Regiomontanus *Ephemerides*, then made widely available by the recent advent of printing, showed both the full moon and the

Mars-moon conjunction on May 8, and a position for the conjunction just over Scorpio 17°, certainly within the poetic accuracy of "degrees twice nine."

The astrological expression "Lord of the year" at first troubled us because it is not very precisely defined, but ultimately it helped clinch our case. We assumed that Skelton must have accepted some definition deriving from the ancient *Tetrabiblos* of Ptolemy. The seventeeth-century astrologer Henry Coley, still working within the Ptolemiac tradition, gave a recipe for finding the strongest planet for a particular year, that is, the "Lord of the year." His scheme called for erecting the planetary configurations at the times of the sun's ingress into the four cardinal points (Aries, Cancer, Libra, and Capricorn), examining the relative strengths of the planets, "and that Planet so qualified shall be the chief Ruler, or *Almuten* for that Revolution, or Lord of the Year; and tis the most Rational way to Elect him so" (Coley, 1676, p. 26).

Since Coley observed that "It seems to me most convenient and natural in the judgment of annual events to assume four beginnings . . . and so give judgment of the state of the spring quarter from the beginning of Aries," we restricted our attention to the planetary configurations at the time when the sun enters Aries. For this we used the old printed *Ephemerides* of Regiomontanus rather than the modern calculations, because it was more important to know when Skelton thought that the sun entered Aries than when it actually did. At the time of the vernal equinox in 1495, Mars was in Scorpio, its zodiacal sign or domicile, as well as being in a mildly favorable house. No other planet was in its own domicile, and any properties that a fifteenth-century astrologer would have found propitious for the other planets were offset or weakened by unfavorable aspects. Thus, in May 1495, Mars was undoubtedly "Lord of the Year." By the same procedure, 1523 was clearly ruled out.

Why, then, with Mars in such strength in 1495 does he "put up his sword, for he could make no war"? The astrological synopsis prefaced to the Regiomontanus *Ephemerides* sheds further light on the poetic phrase with the warning, "When Mars is in conjunction with the moon, avoid soldiers and strong men; flee from quarrels." The moon, a nocturnal symbol of femininity, was thus binding the masculine Mars in Scorpio, his nocturnal house; likewise his retrogression and opposition with the sun weakened his power. With poetic economy, Skelton had listed the prime horoscopic elements that cast their peaceful influence on the guiding star of a military man. And, as Tucker promptly realized, the allegorical meaning applied well to the Anglo-Scottish relations of 1495, particularly relevant for a poem written at a castle in the Border Country.

By proposing that the poem was written around the mid 1490s rather than nearer to the 1523 publication date as the earlier critics had thought, the poem fits well with Skelton's laureation at the Universities of Oxford (1488), Louvain (1492), and Cambridge (1493). In its inception then, it might have been Skelton's cockcrow over his rights to the laurel and a demonstration of his poetic prowess. As it happened, the poem was neither finished nor published for nearly three decades.

Our revision of the Skelton chronology (Gingerich and Tucker, 1969) was sufficiently radical that not all of the Skeltonian scholars have accepted it with enthusiasm. Nevertheless, at least the standard Oxford edition of Skelton's works now takes cognizance of these suggestions.

John Donne and the Continental Astronomers

A third English writer with fascinating astronomical connections is John Donne. A poet and churchman of Stuart times, Donne lived three centuries after Chaucer and a century after Skelton. In 1610, when Donne wrote an elegy in memory of Elizabeth Drury, a child whom he had never seen, Galileo had just published his *Siderieus nuncius* containing the first telescopic observations of the heavens, and Kepler had published his *Astronomia nova* with its discovery of the elliptical orbits of the planets. Probably Donne knew of both these astronomers when he wrote his poem, *The First Anniversary*; it reflects the strong turbulence of change as the Aristotelian philosophy crumbled:

> And new Philosophy cals all in doubt,
> The Element of fire is quite put out;
> The Sunne is lost, and th'earth, and no mans wit
> Can well direct him, where to looke for it.

Donne continues

> We thinke the heauens enjoy their Sphericall
> Their round proportion embracing all.
> But yet their various and perplexed course,
> Obseru'd in diuers ages doth enforce
> Men to finde out so many Eccentrique parts,
> Such diuers downe-right lines, such ouerthwarts,
> As disproportion that pur forme. It teares
> The Firmament in eight and fortie sheeres,
> And in those constellations there arise
> New starres, and old do vanish from our eyes.

Donne's graphic description of the changing philosophical framework includes the specific astronomical observation that "There arise new stars, and old do vanish from our eyes." The line suggests that Donne had something specific in mind; undoubtedly the spectacular nova of 1604 described by Kepler in a lengthy volume, *De stella nova.*

In fact, we know for sure that Donne had access to Kepler's book, because early in 1611 Donne published anonymously an attack on the Jesuits entitled *Ignatius His Conclave*, at the beginning of which he mentions both Galileo and Kepler. He writes, "I thinke it an honester part as yet to be silent, then to do *Galileo* wrong by speaking of it, who of late hath summoned the other worlds, the Stars to come neerer to him, and give him an account of themselves. Or to Keppler, who (as himselfe testifies of himselfe) *ever since* Tycho Braehe's *death, hath received it into his care, that no new thing should be done in heaven without his knowledge.*" In the margin alongside this passage appear the notes "Nuncius Sydereus" and "*De stella in Cygno,*" the title of the third part of Kepler's *De stella nova.*

Although Donne was quoting Kepler's cocky statement almost verbatim, the German astronomer felt annoyed at his minor inclusion in a satire set primarily in hell, and he complained in his posthumously published *Somnium.* In his eighth note to this pioneering piece of science fiction, Kepler remarked, "I suppose a copy of this little work fell into the hands of the author of the bold satire entitled *Ignatius His Conclave,* where he stings me by name at the very outset. Later on he brings poor Copernicus to Plato's court."

Thus, even at the end of his life, Kepler was apparently still unaware of the identity of the anonymous author of *Ignatius His Conclave.* In fact, Kepler and Donne had actually met in Linz a decade earlier, at the end of October 1619. Donne, by then ordained, was traveling with James Hay, Earl of Doncaster, on a diplomatic mission to the continent, and in the course of their journey through Austria they met the famous astronomer. In an undated letter to an unnamed correspondent, Kepler explained that he had asked a "Doctore Theologo Namens Donne" to carry a dedication copy of his latest work back to James I. Earlier German scholars, missing the significance of Donne's name, had supposed that the book was the *De stella nova,* especially since Kepler's inscribed copy to King James is still preserved in the British Library, and, thus, that the letter was written around 1606. Actually, however, as Wilbur Applebaum (1971) has pointed out, the meeting with Donne was later in Kepler's life and the book must have been the *Harmonice mundi,* a work that was actually dedicated to the English monarch. However long Donne and Kepler remained in conversation, they apparently did not touch on the fact that Donne was the anonymous author of *Ignatius His Conclave,* with its fleeting reference to Kepler.

In Sir Geoffrey Keynes's *A Bibliography of Dr. John Donne* (1973), there is appended a list of books known from Donne's library. It includes the current location of a single Keplerian volume, his *Eclogae Chronicae* of 1615, and no other astronomy books at all. Did John Donne himself own a copy of Galileo's *Siderieus nuncius?* And did Kepler press into Donne's hands a copy of the *Harmonice mundi* when they met in Linz in 1619?

Several years ago, when I was on the trail of some copies of Copernicus's *De revolutionibus,* I accidentally stumbled across Donne's own copy of Kepler's *De stella nova.* In the John Rylands Library in Manchester I was trying to untangle several crossed-out signatures in their second edition *De revolutionibus.* I sought help, and the librarians pointed out a provenance file that listed the names of previous owners of early books in their collection. While leafing through the file books, my eye caught the name of John Donne. Pausing, I realized the book was none other than Kepler's account of the Nova of 1604. Needess to say, I took a look at the book itself. Donne's clearly recognizable signature appears on the title page, but, disappointingly, the work is otherwise unannotated.

What about copies of the *Sidereus nuncius* or the *Harmonice mundi* with Donne's signature? Quite possibly such treasures are still lurking unnoticed in some library or private collection. Perhaps some serendipitous transdisciplinary intersections will some day bring forth further connections between this English poet and the continental astronomers.

References

Altick, R. D. *The Scholar Adventurers*. New York: Macmillan, 1960.

Applebaum, W. "Donne's Meeting with Kepler: A Previously Unknown Episode." *Philological Quarterly*, 1971, *50*, 132–134.

Coley, H. *Clavis Astrologiae Elimata: or a Key to the Whole Art of Astrology*. London: Tooke and Tho. Sawbridge, 1676.

Curry, W. C. *Chaucer and the Medieval Sciences*. London: Allen and Unwin, 1960.

Gingerich, O., and Tucker, M. J. "The Astronomical Dating of Skelton's Garland of Laurel." *Huntington Library Quarterly*, 1969, *32*, 207–220.

Keynes, G. L. *A Bibliography of Dr. John Donne*. (4th ed.) Cambridge: Cambridge University Press, 1973.

Kinsman, R. S. *John Skelton: Poems*. Oxford: Oxford University Press, 1969.

Manley, F. *John Donne: The Anniversaries*. Baltimore: Johns Hopkins University Press, 1963.

North, J. D. "Kalenderes Enlumyned Ben They." *The Review of English Studies*, 1969, *20*, 129–154, 257–283, 418–444.

Price, D. J. *The Equatorie of the Planetis*. Cambridge: Cambridge University Press, 1969.

Robinson, F. N. (Ed.). *The Works of Geoffrey Chaucer*. (2nd ed.) Boston: Houghton Mifflin, 1957.

Owen Gingerich is professor of Astronomy and History of Science at Harvard University, and an astrophysicist at the Smithsonian Astrophysical Observatory in Cambridge. He has nearly completed an annotated census of all known copies of Copernicus's De revolutionibus (1543–1566) *and he is currently editing the twentieth-century volume of the* General History of Astronomy.

Interdisciplinary study must proceed with care. The assertion that Shakespeare's Prospero is an example of the Renaissance scientist does violence to the play, and, more damaging, presents a picture of the early scientist-as-magician that can distort our understanding of science in the seventeenth century.

Prospero and the Renaissance Scientist

Barbara A. Mowat

Jacob Bronowski, in a posthumously published essay, notes that great ages in science and the arts usually coincide. Galileo and Shakespeare, he points out, were born in the same year, "grew into greatness in the same age," and "when Galileo was looking through his telescope at the moon, Shakespeare was writing *The Tempest*" (1977, p. 29). Bronowski does not urge any closer relationship between Shakespeare and Renaissance science than the mere fact of the coincidence of these scientific and literary peaks, but other writers would like to place Shakespeare, and *The Tempest* in particular, within the development of science as it was practiced in the early seventeenth century. Dame Frances Yates (1975, p. 96) was probably the first to see Shakespeare's Prospero as a type of the Renaissance "magus as scientist," but she is not alone in linking Prospero to John Dee (for instance, French, 1972; Deacon, 1968) and in seeing Prospero as "the ideal type of Hermetic scientist" (Kearney, 1971, p. 41). As Prospero's reputation as a scientist spreads, he is linked not only to Dee, but also to Giordano Bruno and to Leonardo da Vinci (Kott, 1964; Yates, 1969), and one expects any day to find articles tying him to Kepler, Gilbert, or even Bacon. Since all of these scientists were influenced by magic traditions, such analogies seem, on the surface, plausible.

I also find this image of Prospero as a magus-scientist an attractive one. When Kearney (1971), in describing the science of the sixteenth and seven-

A. White (Ed.). *New Directions for Teaching and Learning: Interdisciplinary Teaching*, no. 8.
San Francisco: Jossey-Bass, December 1981

teenth centuries, claims Prospero as "the ideal type of the Hermetic scientist bringing justice and peace to a disturbed world" (p. 41), I would like to take this claim as valid. It lifts Prospero's magic from the realm of the demonic, the suspect, the medieval, and makes it admirable and accessible to the twentieth-century mind. Unfortunately, though, the text will not support such a claim. Prospero is not drawn as a Renaissance scientist — Hermetic or Rosicrucian — and to so label him is both to misread the play and to distort the figure of the scientist as he existed in the early seventeenth century.

Prospero is many things: He is an ousted duke, an intellectual, and a magician with roots in a variety of magic traditions. His language sometimes reminds us of the influential sixteenth-century magus, Cornelius Agrippa:

> . . . being transported
> And rapt in secret studies . . .
> . . . all dedicated
> To closeness and the bettering of my mind . . . .
> [*The Tempest* I, ii, 76–77, 89–90]

Sometimes he speaks for wizards and conjurers through the ages:

> . . . I have bedimmed
> The noontide sun, called forth the mutinous winds,
> And 'twixt the green sea and the azured vault
> Set roaring war . . . . Graves at my command
> Have waked their sleepers, oped, and let 'em forth
> By my so potent Art.
> [*The Tempest* V, i, 41–50]

And sometimes, especially in his dealings with Ariel and his staging of a disappearing banquet, he reminds us vividly of the street magicians with their boy apprentices who entertained the gullible at street fairs and in theater variety shows. Within the figure of Prospero, Shakespeare has managed to capture the power, the glamour, and the hocus-pocus that attends always on the magician, and has managed thus to comment intriguingly on the nature of illusion — magical illusion, poetic illusion, and theatrical illusion (Mowat, 1981). But I can find nothing in the text that would seriously link Prospero to Renaissance science, and I am increasingly puzzled by references to his "magico-scientific knowledge" (Yates, 1975, p. 96).

The fact that Prospero is now being seen as a scientist is, I think, an aberration of intellectual history. Until recently, few were willing to face the fact that the great Renaissance scientists were still deeply influenced by occult traditions — that Kepler believed in astrology and cast horoscopes (Mandrou, 1978; Thomas, 1971), that Gilbert saw magnetism as "best understood in terms of an animistic force" (Debus, 1978, p. 89), that Copernicus was influenced by Hermeticism and Newton by alchemical lore (Yates, 1969; Dobbs, 1975). Now the pendulum has swung. Not only are we shown that even Francis Bacon was deeply influenced by magic (Rossi, 1968), but we are urged to go a step further and equate Renaissance magic with Renaissance science. Many writings about the period tempt one to do so. Eugenio Garin (1969), writing about "Magic and Astrology in the Civilization of the Renaissance," makes one want to believe that science and magic are one: "First, all sciences, insofar as they inquire into the structure of reality, are subservient to magic, for magic is a practical activity which aims at the transformation of nature by interfering with the laws of nature through technical knowledge of how they operate" (p. 146).

This equation of magic with science to which we wish to give our assent lies behind the "scientific" interpretation of *The Tempest*. The fact that Prospero depends upon his books, that he draws his influence from the stars, that he rules over a world filled with spirits, and that he uses his powers to good ends — these facts have seemed enough for several writers to place him as "another John Dee" — a re-creation of the happy Elizabethan conjoining of conjuring with scientific experimentation, and a prefiguring of the Newton whose cold scientific visage hid a mind lost on the trackless seas of the occult.

Although scientists from Dee to Newton willingly explored the "occult" as well as the "permissible" approaches to knowledge, one of the facts ignored in the equation of Renaissance magic with Renaissance science is that they did so in a search for truth. I am hesitant to generalize even this much about "the Renaissance scientist." Bacon's search seems very different from Kepler's; Kepler's "truth" seems different from Tycho's; and all of these figures seem a world apart from Galileo. Yet, even with John Dee, an admitted converser with spirits, one sees clearly in his writings that the occult was, for him, only another window into mathematical, scientific, and philosophical truth (Heilbron, 1978). He turned to crystal balls and angels only after he felt he had exhausted all other means of finding answers to his essentially scientific questions. He was an indefatigable searcher after knowledge, an early supporter of Copernicus, and one of England's leading mathematician-philosophers (Johnson, 1937). Prospero is like Dee only in his love of his books and in his belief in human contact with spirits. That is, he shares with Dee only those "magical" qualities that for Dee were tools for the advancement of knowledge, but which, for Prospero, are ends in themselves, or ends by which he can reclaim political power and family status.

The distinction is a significant one. Figures did exist in the Renaissance who sought to use magic for personal power or spiritual growth or dominance; some such magicians were, like Agrippa and like Prospero, linked to Hermetic lore; others, like Sycorax (the witch whom Prospero replaces) were linked to the demonic. But figures like Kepler, Dee, Gilbert, and Bacon clung to magic traditions not out of a desire for personal power or even personal growth, but because these traditions seemed to continue to give correct answers to their questions. Behind their search for power over nature was an overriding belief in shared knowledge, in the worth of the mechanical arts, and in the value of a slowly and carefully built structure of insight into the workings of nature (Rossi, 1968; Mandrou, 1978; Heilbron 1978; Johnson 1937).

The focus of *The Tempest* has almost nothing to do with shared insight into nature's structure, shared concerns about the cosmos, or shared beliefs about the interrelatedness of the mechanical arts, scientific theory, and the future welfare of mankind. These were common concerns of the English Renaissance scientist, whether at Gresham College or in the informal "academies" that finally culminated in the Royal Society (Johnson, 1937). They were accessible to Shakespeare either through his son-in-law, John Hall, or in court or London circles. But the emphasis of *The Tempest* is elsewhere.

We can get some sense of the emphasis, and of the absence of scientific concerns in the play, if we look briefly at the period during which Shakespeare was writing *The Tempest*. We can date that period with unusual precision, because some of the documents that Shakespeare read before writing the play were not available until the summer of 1610, and because the play was performed in November of 1611 (Bullough, 1975). These months coincide with a period in England's history unusually rich in scientific interest. During this period, Galileo's *Siderieus nuncius* reached London, along with at least one of his telescopes; Kepler's *De stella nova* (1608) was already known, and, in 1610, his *Conversations with Galileo* was published, and Tycho Brahe's *Progymnasmata* was reissued. There is abundant evidence that these works were known immediately in England, and that they caused tremendous intellectual excitement. English diplomats and scientists wrote enthusiastically about the discoveries and their implications (Johnson, 1937; Coffin, 1958), and English scientists "were not only fully abreast of all the latest developments . . . but were also carrying on independent researches of their own along similar lines" (Johnson, 1937, p. 229). Francis Bacon seems to have learned of the telescopic discoveries during these same months, and by 1612 had written two works on the science of stellar motion (Rossi, 1968). Since James I received a copy of Kepler's *De stella nova*, inscribed to him by the author (Johnson, 1937), and a copy of Galileo's *Siderieus nuncius,* mailed to him by Wotton on the day of its publication in March 1610 (Coffin, 1958), the new discoveries certainly reached court circles. Even in the universities, bastions of scholastic approaches to knowledge, the new telescopic discoveries made an instant impact. In 1611, only a year after Galileo's book had raised the question of the inhabitability of the moon, "one of the questions set forth for disputation . . . by the incepting masters at Oxford was 'An luna sit habitabilis?'" (Johnson, 1937, p. 241).

Rather than linger over the multiple interrelations of the English scientists and their compeers in Florence, Padua, and Prague during this time of intellectual ferment, let me simply note that the keen interest in cosmological theory felt in England since the days of Dee, Recorde, Digges, and Gilbert surged into new prominence with the almost simultaneous discoveries of Galileo and Kepler—and this during the very months in which Shakespeare was writing *The Tempest*. In 1611, while Shakespeare writes of Prospero, John Donne writes wittily of "Galileo, . . . who of late hath summoned the other worlds, the Stars to come neerer to him, and give him an account of themselves" and of "Keppler, who (as himselfe testifies to himselfe) ever since Tycho Brahe's death hath received it into his care, that no new things should be done in heaven without his knowledge" (Donne, 1952, p. 319). During the crucial months of 1610–1611, Donne reveals in poem after poem his knowledge of all the new cosmological writings and his awareness of their implications (Coffin, 1958), sometimes despairing over the shift of the center from earth to sun and sometimes mocking man's training of the telescope on the stars: "Loth . . . to labour thus / To goe to heaven, we make heaven come to us" (Donne, 1952, p. 193).

To turn from Galileo's excited prose, from letters written by English scientists in 1610 claiming that "Me thinkes my diligent Galileus hath done more in his three fold discoverie than Magellane in opening the streightes to the South sea" (Johnson, 1937, p. 228), and from John Donne's numerous accounts of the impact of the New Philosophy to the contemporary *Tempest* is to feel momentarily disoriented. One has not stepped back in time or out of time. In terms of geographical and intellectual journeys, the play is clearly a product of the early seventeenth century. Voyage literature published during the months of 1610–1611 pervades the play, and we are clearly in a world of rediscovery of the classics, as incidents from *The Aeneid* jostle classical mythology for prominence of place (Mowat, 1977). But scientific excitement about the new cosmology is simply not present, nor is there any sense of the new attitude toward the work of the scientist heralded by *Bacon's Advancement of Learning* (1605) and demonstrated by the cooperation of English, Italian, and Northern European scientists during the years we are here considering.

Paolo Rossi has demonstrated Francis Bacon's grounding in the alchemical tradition in part by showing linguistic affinities between Bacon's writings and the language of the alchemists. The linguistic affinities of *The Tempest* (and the story told in *The Tempest*) lead us not to alchemy or to cosmology, but rather to the old familiar story of the sea voyage that turns out to be a new discovery of the self. Prospero, the central figure, has been ousted from his dukedom in a coup d 'état engineered by his brother Antonio and a neighbor king, Alonso. A student of the liberal arts, Prospero had left the government to his brother, had been captured in the coup, and had, with his baby daughter, been put out to sea to die. He had reached land, had used his books to perfect his magic powers, had gained control over a powerful spirit, subjugated a monster (the offspring of the devil and a witch), and had raised his daughter with great care. Twelve years later, when the play opens, Fortune has brought all his enemies to his island. Through his "prescience," he knows that his future prosperity hangs "upon a most auspicious star" whose influence he must now court or "ever after droop." Wearing his magic robe and operating through his spirit servant, he wrecks the ships, brings the passengers to shore, brings together his daughter and the prince of Naples, convicts the king of his sin for aiding the coup, recovers his dukedom, and brings about the marriage of his daughter and the prince. In the process of the action, he uses magic to charm swords, to put people to sleep, to present visions — wonderful or horrible — to various characters, and to madden and then make sane his chief enemies. He then renounces his magic, sets his spirit servant free, and asks the prayers of the audience as he sets sail for Milan, where every "third thought" will be of his grave.

As countless critics have noticed, the play is permeated with sea-words and sea-sounds, with echoes from Virgil, and language from new world voyagers (for instance, Brower, 1951; Frey, 1979; Brockman, 1966). The play is about human experience altered by the strangeness of a magic environment, but altered only in intensity. The basic passions explored are young love, remorse, anger, despair, greed, and joy; the meditations are on death and prayer. The shipwreck on the seemingly desert island brings forth dialogue on proper civilization, on power and on man's ultimate powerlessness; on Providence, Destiny, kindness, and cruelty. The play, then, in spite of its magical setting, is intensely human: A wedding masque presented by spirits acting the parts of classical goddesses is preceded by a lecture on the dangers of premarital sex and interrupted by the sudden anger of the magician at his failure to educate his adopted monster. The magician himself is all too human: anxious, easily angered, and often unlikeable.

The play has much to say to us about proper rulership; about relationships between the colonizer and the colonized; and about guilt, vengefulness, and forgiveness. It has almost nothing to say about scientific — or even magical — control of nature. When the stars are mentioned, they are simply astrological wielders of power over man's fate. Instead of a discussion of the newly pressing questions about the inhabitability of the moon, we find instead the old superstitious notion of "the man in the moon," used in the play, as by white men in the New World, as a way of playing on the primitive beliefs and fears of gullible natives. In three of the most famous speeches of the play, where Prospero-as-scientist could have given us a clear indication of his interest in cosmology, in vitalism, or in other current scientific debates or discoveries, we find, instead, a mystical meditation on the insubstantiality of the physical world — a "baseless fabric" which will dissolve into air, into thin air" (IV. i); we find a wizard-speech in which the magician attributes his power to elves, and in which he vows to "drown his book" and give up his "rough magic" (V, i); and we find, finally an epilogue in which Prospero echoes not the language of the new science or of Hermeticism, but of the church and the Bible:

> Now my charms are all o'erthrown
> And what power I have's mine own
> Which is most faint . . . .

Now I want
Spirits to enforce, art to enchant;
And my ending is despair
Unless I be relieved by prayer
Which pierces so, that it assaults
Mercy itself, and frees all faults.
As you from crimes would pardon'd be
Let your indulgence set me free.
[*The Tempest*, Epilogue, 1–3, 13–20]

I do not agree with Murray (1948) that Shakespeare was not a "Renaissance man." *The Tempest* reflects a world that is opening to wonderful new geographical discoveries, that is beginning to question the power of the king, and that is beginning to look at itself in the light of the new worlds and new peoples it is discovering; the play resonates with the old world of classical voyages and mythologies rediscovered in the Renaissance. But the new sense of excitement about the cosmos, the new sense of man's centrality promulgated by Hermeticism and Renaissance science alike—these are absent from *The Tempest*. And to try to claim Prospero as the type of the Renaissance scientist who "uses his magico-scientific powers for good" (Yates, 1975, p. 94) is to do violence to the play and, perhaps more damaging, to present a picture of the Renaissance scientist-as-magician—complete with magic robes, wands, and spells—that seriously distorts a proper understanding of science in the early seventeenth century.

References

Brockman, P. "*The Tempest*: Conventions of Art and Empire." In J. R. Brown and B. Harris (Eds.), *Later Shakespeare*. Stratford-upon-Avon Studies, No. 8. London: Edward Arnold, 1966.

Bronowski, J. *A Sense of the Future: Essays in Natural Philosophy*. Cambridge, Mass.: M.I.T. Press, 1977.

Brower, R. *The Fields of Light*. New York: Oxford University Press, 1951.

Bullough, G. *Narrative and Dramatic Sources of Shakespeare*. Vol. VIII: *The Romances*. London: Routledge and Kegan Paul, 1975.

Coffin, C. M. *John Donne and the New Philosophy*. New York: The Humanities Press, 1958.

Deacon, R. *John Dee: Scientist, Geographer, Astrologer, and Secret Agent to Elizabeth I*. London: Frederick Muller, 1968.

Debus, A. G. *Man and Nature in the Renaissance*. Cambridge History of Science Series. Cambridge: Cambridge University Press, 1978.

Dobbs, B. J. T. *The Foundations of Newton's Alchemy: or, "The Hunting of the Greene Lyon"*. New York: Cambridge University Press, 1975.

Donne, J. *The Complete Poetry and Selected Prose*. In M. Coffin (Ed.), New York: Modern Library, 1952.

French, P. *John Dee: The World of an Elizabethan Magus*. London: Routledge and Kegan Paul, 1972.

Frey, C. "*The Tempest* and the New World." *Shakespeare Quarterly*, 1979, *30* (1), 29–41.

Garin, E. *Science and Civic Life in the Italian Renaissance*. (B. Munz, trans.) Anchor Books. New York: Doubleday, 1969.

Heilbron, J. L. "Dee and the Scientific Revolution." In W. Shumaker (Ed. and trans.), *John Dee on Astronomy. Propaedeumata Aphoristica (1558 and 1568) Latin and English*. Berkeley: University of California Press, 1978.

Johnson, F. R. *Astronomical Thought in Renaissance England*. Baltimore, Md.: Johns Hopkins University Press, 1937.

Kearney, H. F. *Science and Change 1500–1700*. New York: McGraw-Hill, 1971.

Kott, J. *Shakespeare Our Contemporary*. (B. Taborski, trans.) London: Methuen, 1964.

Mandrou, R. *From Humanism to Science 1480–1700*. (B. Pearce, trans.) Vol. III: *The Pelican History of European Thought*. Suffolk: Pelican Books, 1978.

Mowat, B. A. "'And that's true too': Structures and Meanings in *The Tempest*." In Donovan, D. and DeNeef, L. (Eds.), *Renaissance Papers 1976*. Southeastern Renaissance Conference, 1977, 37–50.

Mowat, B. A. "Prospero, Agrippa, and Hocus Pocus." *English Literary Renaissance*, Fall 1981.

Murray, J. M. *Shakespeare*. London: Jonathan Cape, 1948.

Rossi, P. *Francis Bacon: From Magic to Science*. (Sacha Rabinovitch, trans.) Chicago: University of Chicago Press, 1968.

Thomas, K. *Religion and the Decline of Magic*. New York: Scribner's, 1971.

Yates, F. A. *Giordano Bruno and the Hermetic Tradition*. New York: Random House, 1969.

Yates, F. A. *Shakespeare's Last Plays: A New Approach*. London: Routledge and Kegan Paul, 1975.

Barbara A. Mowat, Hollifield Professor of English at Auburn University, has written primarily about Shakespeare. She is also coeditor of an interdisciplinary journal, The Southern Humanities Review, *and is director and coordinator of an interdisciplinary program based on Jacob Bronowski's* Ascent of Man.

Utilizing renewable natural energies as a basis for designing the built environment provides paradigms for a holistic approach to the realities of the postindustrial world in which natural models assert once more their primacy over the artificial.

Toward an Energic Architecture

Carl H. Hertel

The current planetary energy crisis creates a context for reexamining characteristic responses and attitudes toward the energic aspects of being-in-the-world. In the United States, where a small percentage of the world's population consumes a disproportionately large share of the world's energy, we are individually and collectively being required to review values and practices that were predicated on fallacious assumptions about unlimited supplies of energy in the form of petroleum and other fossil fuels. It would appear that we have reached the point on a biological life cycle S-curve, cited by Henderson (1976), at which maximal growth gives way to maintenance, competition gives way to cooperation, and exploitation of the ecosystem is transformed into recycling and restoration. Responses from the establishment to this state of affairs have been banal, inadequate, and regressive (not to mention dangerous; for example, nuclear power plants). What is required exceeds the need for discovering revolutionary new fuels and/or reduction of dependencies upon the automobile and electric hair dryers. What is at issue is the conversion of a cultural disposition to value the artificial above all else into a planetary conciousness that accepts the dynamics of the natural energy flows governing the biosphere.

The human disregard of natural energy flows in favor of artificial technological surrogates is nowhere more evident that in the design and construction of the environmental interventions (so called architecture) of industrial-urban societies. While the reasons and motivations underlying the obsessive

A. White (Ed.). *New Directions for Teaching and Learning: Interdisciplinary Teaching*, no. 8.
San Francisco: Jossey-Bass, December 1981

artificiality of our architecture are exceedingly complex, it is interesting to note that there is ample evidence that the human species (like many others) is genetically imbued with the knowledge and behaviors appropriate to ecologically sound place-making, that is, natural architecture. It seems that deviations characterized as losses of natural knowledge have perverted the place-making process with calamitous results for the species and the planet. Contemporary analysts such as Roszak (1979) suggest that the antidote lies in the personalization of responsibilities for being-in-the-world in order to restore the natural knowledge and wisdom required for survival. The ramifications of such a thesis are far-reaching from the perspective of the dominant culture in America today. This chapter will focus on the role that can be played by the utilization of natural energies (sun, wind, water, biomass, ocean thermal, and geothermal) as a basis for giving form to our environmental interventions in restoring the kinds of natural knowledge we have lost. While we do not deny that the built environment is in some ways an expression of culture, our argument gives greatest credence to the fact that just as "we are what we eat," we are also determined by "where we eat, live, work, and play." From this point of view, the manner in which we "make our places" on the planet suggests a modus operandi for a quiet revolution from the hyperindustrial to the postindustrial phases of our biocultural evolution.

This chapter will consider three principles that are paramount in utilizing natural energies as a basis for giving form to the built environment: (1) the bodily paradigm, (2) a sense of place, and (3) simplicity and flexibility. While these principles are hardly novel, the virulent toxicity of the modern industrial-urban environment suggests they have become divorced from practice. As noted earlier, the current energy crisis serves as an opportunity to reinstate the practice of such principles in striving to achieve an energy-efficient environment while simultaneously redressing the excesses of technological artificiality that threaten the ecological stability of the planet.

The Primacy of the Bodily Paradigm

The fact that the human organism itself is a solar energy system within a solar energy system is the starting point for the realization of natural energies as form determinants in creating the built environment. From this perspective, energy is understood as personal as well as a part of an interrelated macrocosmic system. In such a context, the popular attitude toward energy as something one "obtains" from a gas pump or electrical outlet is dispelled. Furthermore, the bodily paradigm for energy becomes the model for an energic architecture compatible with natural energy flows. Such a model has been the basis for much of the world's architecture in the past. It is beyond the scope of this chapter to suggest precisely how this model was lost to modern architecture. (There are, of course, notable exceptions; for example, Frank Lloyd Wright.) Suffice it to say, the evidence indicates that rapid technological developments engendered by worldwide warfare provided the basis for the dehumanization of our built environment (among many other aspects of our being-in-the-world).

Ordinary language still suggests the vestiges of the image of the built environment in the image of the body. For example, we speak of "the heart of the city." Historically, scholarly research, such as that by Schwaller de Lubicz (1977), documents intensive and sophisticated application of the bodily paradigm in deriving forms of traditional, cosmological architecture in ancient Egypt and elsewhere. Perhaps the clearest expression of the bodily paradigm is seen in the house and village forms of preindustrial peoples such as the Dogon in the sub-Sahara. The work of van Eyck and others (1968), following in the footsteps of Marcel Griaule, demonstrates how the forms of traditional Dogon villages are constructed and perceived as concrete images of the human male and female bodies, creating a kind of biological cosmogony in built form. History, then, demonstrates that the bodily paradigm is the basis for an esthetic that underlies the forms of the human built environment in diverse circumstances, places, and periods. Ezra Pound (1936, p. 23) tells us that such an esthetic sees the natural world filled with "homologies, sympathies, and identities (without which) thought would have been starved and language (art and architecture) chained to the obvious." Needless to say, the logical archetype (natural homology) for the dwelling place is the human body. In periods of history such as our own, when the technological assumes primary importance, poetics such as Pound's are sacrificed to technique (see also Ellul, 1964). From this follows the virtual loss of the bodily paradigm in all but the personalized, vernacular architecture of modern industrial-urban societies. The archetype for form in the built environment of our time has become the machine (the artificial) rather than the human body (the organic). In the context of the current energy crisis, Stein (1978) has demonstrated that one result of this shift of models from the natural to the artificial has been intensive energy inefficiency in typical built forms. In broader terms, another result of this shift has been the loss of "feeling at home" for humans who inhabit the built environment. That is, the impersonality of the technically inspired environment has destroyed the sense of place characterizing earlier architecture. This is perhaps the most debilitating loss of all for the inhabitants of the world's industrial countries.

The Importance of a Sense of Place

Much of the recent writing about place carries strong humanistic leanings that support the notion that the experience of place in natural and man-made settings can best be regarded as esthetic, that is, as a kind of transcending experience. The fiction of Lawrence Durrell (for example, *The Alexandria Quartet*) demonstrates how landscape can be more important than characters; places more important than people. Indeed, Durrell admits (1971) to a belief that human beings are expressions of their landscape. He sees what he calls "the spirit of place" as analogous to those qualities of a vineyard environment that give a particular essence to the wines produced from the grapes grown there. He goes on to suggest that a truly intimate knowledge of a landscape must be perceived with all the senses combined with the reception of a "whispered message" asked by all landscapes: "I am watching you — are you watching yourself in me?" (p. 158).

In architectural writing the essence of place is often seen to lie in a quality of being "here" rather than "there." More often than not, this distinction is made with reference to man-made structures and also suggests "inside" and "outside" as important place-making elements in forming the built environment (Rapoport, 1972). Architecture theoretically places a high value upon the human element in place-making. As van Eyck and others state (1968, pp. 90-92), "What we need is to be at home — wherever we are. As long as it is perpetually somewhere else there will be no question of participation. Architecture, therefore, need do no more than assist man's 'homecoming' . . . . I like to think of it (architecture) as the constructed counter-form of perpetual homecoming." Scholars of comparative religion and anthropology likewise make interesting cases for place as the lack of homogeneity in space. Eliade (1959) sees place as the valorization of the world effected by interruptions or breaks in space denoting that "some parts of space are qualitatively different from others." His image of space becoming place in traditional (religious) societies is that of cosmos/world (as differentiated from chaos which lacks qualitatively different spaces) centered around one image or another of the axis mundi which serves as a medium of communication with the transcendent. He states: "It follows that every construction or fabrication has the cosmogony as paradigmatic model. The creation of the world becomes archetype of every creative human gesture, whatever its plan of reference may be" (p. 45). By the way of contrast, in some societies man-made structures do not play a significant role in place-making. The Australian aborigines are a spectacular example of this tendency according to Rapoport (1972) who notes that: "In general terms it appears that aborigines define place through sacred directions, routes of the dreamtime ancestors, and their stopping places which become sacred sites, landscape features, and the like. Thus, an apparently featureless landscape may become full of meaning and significance, legends, and happenings — that is, full of places" (p. 3-3-8).

From the sociological point of view, Ellis (1972) has developed the interesting and useful term "charisma of place." It refers to the process by which a certain space becomes a place through charisma generated by the "heat" of social distress which causes the annealing of an event, an ideology, and certain physical attributes of the setting. As he and Black (1972) point out, there are many such transformations of urban spaces into vital places in ghetto environments. For example, the street as the "living room" of a community.

The element of place is extremely important to the process of natural energies serving as a basis for giving form to the built environment. Perhaps, it goes without saying that, in addition to the esthetic, humanistic, religious, psychological, and sociological elements noted earlier, it is absolutely necessary in utilizing natural energies to possess an intimate knowledge of a site's particular climate and terrain combined with an awareness of the dynamics of the solar system related to the function of the environmental intervention being constructed. However, it should be noted that this is not necessarily a matter of "technical knowledge" since such knowledge (awareness or sensitivity) has been shown to exist in various species from termites to humans (see von Frisch, 1974). This knowledge is commonly conceived of as "natural wisdom." Forms emanating from such natural wisdom invariably manifest the third principle we are to discuss, that is, simplicity and flexibility.

The Necessity of Simplicity and Flexibility

Lao Tzu (Bynner, 1962, p. 70) tells us, "My way is so simple, so easy to apply/ that only a few will feel it or apply it." Such is the case with the principal, renewable energies in relationship to giving form to the built environment today. Perhaps the greatest threat to utilizing natural energy technologies as form-givers lies in the tendency of the technological elite to disdain such simple techniques as passive solar space and water heating. Another threat to the utilization of natural energy systems lies in the "desimplification" of solar techniques into complex, high technologies such a solar power satellites that will prolong the current emphasis on the artificial and continue to promulgate maximal growth, intensive competition, and exploitation of the ecosystem through continuation of current patterns of energy use and distribution. By contrast, the natural world provides a model for simplicity and flexibility for energy distribution and use. As Stevens (1974) has elegantly stated, scientists from Heraclitus to modern physicists have struggled with the paradox that in nature all things flow, yet remain the same: "The new water chases out the old, but the pattern remains the same" (p. 53). Thus, simplicity is represented by the relatively few patterns in nature; but change (the flow) denotes flexibility in all natural phenomenon. By extension, Bateson (1972, p. 497) points out that, "Social flexibility is a resource as precious as oil or titanium and must be budgeted in appropriate ways, to be spent (like fat) upon needed change . . . flexibility is to specialization as entropy is to negentropy." Change does not result from specialization. Hence, the growing inappropriateness of our complex, overspecialized built environment divorced from natural models. For example, Knowles has suggested how seldom industrial, urban architectural forms follow natural energy flows. In a recent lecture (1979), he described the Century City Towers in Los Angeles as a notable case in point. He illustrated how the towers not only fail to respond to available solar energy inputs, but likewise fail to take cognizance of the man-made microclimates created by the physical juxtaposition of the structures themselves. Such oblivious architecture is ironic in a country where over 1,000 years ago Native Americans successfully demonstrated the ability, techniques, social organization, and natural wisdom for building large multi-unit structures that were acutely responsive to natural energy flows (see Knowles, 1974, pp. 17–46).

Clearly, the dominant model for form-giving in the design of the built environment in industrial societies is not the natural world. Strangely, we build on the relatively hospitable planet earth as if we were constructing neo-natural environments in a not so hospitable outer space. In such circumstances one of the greatest impediments to successful place-making seems to be planning itself and especially the impossibility of "planned flexibility." Indeed, this problem calls into question the entire planning enterprise as it is currently defined and practiced. A suggestion for solution of such a "planning dilemma" may lie in Bateson's later work (1979) in which he emphasizes the importance of stochastic processes for learning and survival. It is the lack of the stochastic element, or interplay between random and selective processes, that "removes" contemporary planning and designing of the built environment from the natural world. That is, planning, as presently practiced, lacks entropy, and hence, suffers stress and becomes over complicated, inflexible, and dysfunctional in the natural world.

A return to the principles for designing the built environment suggested here would entail immense social, economic, educational, and political change. A solar society, for example, would have to shift dependencies on remote, impersonal, monolithic corporate and political entities to dependencies on highly personal social organization keyed to solar access and reliance on natural variables such as the weather. Concepts of community, self, shelter, transport, and even human existence itself would necessarily change. We would, to paraphrase Bateson (1979), discover mind in nature (not to mention nature in mind). The resistance to this evolutionary step is very great. Yet, the coming of a kind of cosmic mandate is suggested by the increasing scarcity and impending depletion of nonrenewable fuels together with the demonstrated dangers of nuclear options combined with their monolithic, inflexible, and maladaptive infrastructures for distribution and profit. Responding to such a mandate through development of an energic architecture based on natural models is to recognize the subtleties of mind in nature and ourselves. Most importantly, definitions of knowledge and means of access to knowledge will be redefined to include recognition of areas of sensual and mental awareness to which the prior technological era has been closed. Such transformations will not be accomplished by forcing everyone to live in solar villages, much less mandating solar heating for all swimming pools. Instead, it seems increasingly clear that whatever transformations do occur will be a natural exercise (perhaps somewhat catastrophic) perceived simply: through our bodies and at our place on the planet. Bateson (1979, p. 219) ably describes the simplicity attending the moment of such changes: "A sort of freedom comes from recognizing what is necessarily so. After that is recognized, comes a knowledge of how to act. You can ride a bicycle only after your partly unconcious reflexes acknowledge the laws of its moving equilibrium." Some, of course, will learn faster than others.

References

Bateson, G. *Steps to an Ecology of Mind.* New York: Random House, 1972.

Bateson, G. *Mind and Nature: A Necessary Unity.* New York: Dutton, 1979.

Bynner, W. *The Way of Life According to Lao Tzu.* New York: Capricorn Books, 1962.

Durrell, L. *Spirit of Place.* New York: Dutton, 1971.

Eliade, M. *The Sacred and the Profane.* New York: Harcourt Brace Jovanovich, 1959.

Ellis, W. R., and Black, J. "Planning, Design, and Black Community Style: The Problem of Occasion-Adequate Space." In W. J. Mitchell (Ed.), *Environmental Design: Research and Practice.* Los Angeles: University of California Press, 1972.

Ellul, J. *The Technological Society.* (J. Wilkinson, trans.) New York: Knopf, 1964.

Henderson, H. "Ideologies, Paradigms, and Myths: Changes in Our Operative Social Values." *Liberal Education: The Bulletin of the Association of American Colleges,* 1976, *62* (2), 143–156.

Knowles, R. *Energy and Form: An Ecological Approach to Urban Growth.* Cambridge, Mass.: M.I.T. Press, 1974.

Knowles, R. "Solar Access, Rhythm, and Design." Paper presented at the Pitzer College Solar Colloquium, Claremont, Calif., October 1979.

Pound, E. *The Chinese Written Character as a Medium for Poetry.* San Francisco: City Lights, 1968. (Originally published 1936).

Rapoport, A. "Australian Aborigines and the Definition of Place." In W. J. Mitchell (Ed.), *Environmental Design: Research and Practice.* Los Angeles: University of California Press, 1972.

Roszak, T. *Person/Planet: The Creative Disintegration of Industrial Society.* New York: Doubleday, 1979.

Schwaller de Lubicz, R. A. *The Temple in Man: The Secrets of Ancient Egypt.* (R. Lawlor and D. Lawlor, trans.) Brookline, Mass.: Autumn Press, 1977.

Stein, R. *Architecture and Energy.* New York: Anchor Books, 1978.

Stevens, P. *Patterns in Nature.* Boston: Little, Brown, 1974.

van Eyck, A., and others. "A Miracle of Moderation." In *VIA 1 Ecology in Design.* New York: Grossman, 1968.

von Frisch, K. *Animal Architecture.* (L. Gombrich, trans.) New York: Harcourt Brace Jovanovich, 1974.

Carl H. Hertel is professor of Art and Environmental Design at Pitzer College and the Claremont Graduate School, Claremont, California. He is the coordinator of the Pitzer Solar Colloquium, an interdisciplinary program providing a comprehensive course in solar energy for liberal arts students.

Two poems by a modern scientist-poet exemplify a play of wit and insight not easily held within disciplinary bounds.

Two Poems

Miroslav Holub
translated by Jarmila and Ian Milner

Brief Thoughts on the Theory of Relativity

Albert Einstein, discussing—
　　　　(knowledge is discovering
　　　　what to say)—discussing
　　　　with Paul Valéry,
　　　　was asked:

Mr. Einstein, what do you do
　　　　with your thoughts? Write them down
　　　　immediately they come to you? Or wait
　　　　till evening? Or morning?

Albert Einstein responded:
　　　　Monsieur Valéry, in our craft
　　　　thoughts are so rare
　　　　that when you have one
　　　　you certainly won't forget it

Even a year after.

A. White (Ed.). *New Directions for Teaching and Learning: Interdisciplinary Teaching*, no. 8.
San Francisco: Jossey-Bass, December 1981

Brief Thoughts on Exactness

Fish
       move exactly there and exactly then,
just as
       birds have their inbuilt exact measure of time and place.

But mankind,
       deprived of instinct, is aided
       by scientific research, the essence of which
       this story shows.

A certain soldier
       had to fire a gun every evening exactly at six.
       He did it like a soldier. When his exactness
       was checked, he stated:

I follow
       an absolutely precise chronometer in the shop window
       of the clockmaker downtown. Every day at seventeen
       forty-five I set my watch by it and
       proceed up the hill where the gun stands ready.
       At seventeen fifty-nine exactly I reach the gun
       and exactly at eighteen hours I fire.

It was found
       that this method of firing was absolutely exact.
       There was only the chronometer to be checked.
       The clockmaker downtown was asked about its exactness.

Oh, said the clockmaker,
       this instrument is one of the most exact. Imagine,
       for years a gun has been fired here at six exactly.
       And every day I look at the chronometer
       and it always shows exactly six.

So much for exactness.
       And the fish move in the waters and the heavens are filled
       with the murmur of wings, while

The chronometers tick and the guns thunder.

Miroslav Holub is chief research immunologist of the Institute for Clinical and Experimental Medicine in Prague. He has published thirteen books of poetry and four books of prose and essays. During spring 1979, Holub was guest writer-in-residence at Oberlin College.

*The reception and perception of knowledge are strongly influenced
by the human context. Although our attention in teaching and
learning is often on the facts and techniques, our success
depends upon the human relationships.*

Process and Environment
in Teaching and Learning

Alvin M. White

An experience sometimes has such a profound effect that it leads one to infer
general principles of which the particular experience is an instance. If the
insights are true, then the general illuminates the particular that evoked it.

I shared such a fortunate experience with students at M.I.T. several
years ago. The quiet glow of remembrance still inspires me. The Division for
Study and Research in Education (DSRE) offered me a visiting professorship
and an invitation to lead a seminar of my choice for the 1976 spring term. The
invitation was an opportunity to consider questions that are common to all disciplines, and therefore are studied by very few, if at all. I proposed a series of
questions: How do people obtain knowledge? What are the limits of certainty?
What is the relation between general and scientific knowledge? What is the
role of beauty, simplicity, or intuition in creative discovery? Our present
knowledge in the arts, humanities, and sciences is the legacy of creative imagination. How can this legacy influence education at all levels? Appropriate
readings were suggested. The scope was at once frightening and exhilarating
to me. Being a visitor encourages audaciousness.

There were twelve students. Artificial intelligence, biology, computer
science, electrical engineering, environmental studies, linguistics, mathematics, physics, and visual arts were represented. The group was interdisciplinary
or multidisciplinary. Our experience was transdisciplinary or transcendent!

A. White (Ed.). *New Directions for Teaching and Learning: Interdisciplinary Teaching*, no. 8.
San Francisco: Jossey-Bass, December 1981

We reported on, considered, and discussed the writings of various authors in search of answers. The answers, however, as to how we were obtaining knowledge were, for us, embedded in the process and its context.

We were scheduled to meet twice a week from 9:00 to 10:30 A. M. We quickly found ourselves continuing the discussion until noon. Everyone canceled other morning appointments. Students invited their professors to participate. Visitors to DSRE would ask permission to observe quietly, although their reticence was usually soon overcome. One student remarked that the popularity of our seminar among visitors was probably because openness, honest listening, and caring for each other were evident. Every contribution was accepted in a nonjudgmental way. No one was forced to speak, and everyone had a chance to speak. We examined writings by Dewey, Kant, Polanyi, Popper, Russell, and others.

The last week of the term was a time to discuss and evaluate the seminar. Why was it so successful? What had happened to us? How had we been transformed from strangers to a group of friends and colleagues? It was as if we had chanced upon a semester-long celebration, and, like Alain-Fournier's Wanderer, we had been caught up in the spirit of the place. A student observed that this was the first course where her presence in the room had "made a difference."

Why had the seminar been so remarkably satisfying? What had we learned and what should we do if we wanted to find that spirit of celebration again? An unexpected answer emerged; one that answered some of the questions of the seminar as well as the questions about the seminar. The answer that came from one of the students in a moment of insight was "love and trust."

What did that phrase mean? The concept came from the process of our exploration, not from any of the disciplines represented. Love and trust contributed to the spirit of celebration and were essential ingredients in the process of obtaining knowledge. Some instances were remembered when those ingredients were absent, and then only minimal learning had occurred. Should love and trust have been such a surprising answer? Was my surprise a legacy of my formal education? In the past was I too unseeing to have noticed those qualities, or is my memory influenced by the cruelties and meanness often found in the academic scene? The students and I recognized our experience as real and exceptional. The rarity of such an experience for us made us treasure it. And yet, would such an answer be considered sentimental or worse?

Love and trust seem far removed from mathematical logic or electrical engineering as they are encountered in the classroom. Yet, if we are engaged in learning and teaching, then all of the disciplines share the process involved in intellectual imagination and creation. Love and trust were natural parts of our learning in the group setting. We came together, attracted by the description of the seminar. Some progress toward understanding was made. Our understanding, however, went beyond the seminar. We, perhaps, internalized Erikson's words, "Love is the greatest of human virtues, . . . Care is a quality essential for psychosocial evolution, for we are the teaching species. . . . As (man) transmits the rudiments, will and competence, . . . he conveys a logic much beyond the literal meaning of the words he teaches, and he gradually outlines a particular world image and style of fellowship. . . . We understand that the adult man is so constituted as to need to be needed" (1964, p. 127, 130).

Perhaps my surprise came from the absence of love and trust as explicit items in the syllabus or objectives of any course or table of contents of a text. The syllabus is focused on the discipline. How we obtain knowledge is considered outside of the discipline and therefore is usually not discussed. Traveling on the road, however, is as important as finding the road of knowledge. Presumably, obtaining knowledge is an objective of a course. Why not assume that our seminar was the natural mode and that teaching and learning without love and trust are unnatural? Reflection on that seminar has been an impetus to seek confirmation that the student's insight about our success was an instance of a general principle; that those who adopt this mode are not sentimental, but are natural.

Mathematics is considered by some of the uninitiated to be devoid of any emotional content. By extension, perhaps, the teaching and learning of mathematics may be thought to be independent of emotional content. Recently, however, the concept of Mathematical Anxiety has been recognized (Tobias, 1978). In describing programs to overcome Math Anxiety at Wesleyan, Stanford, and Mills College, the consensus was, notwithstanding any superficial differences in the various approaches, that there was a common element, probably essential to each program's success. That element was the understanding by anxious students that there was someone who could help them, and who had faith in each student's ability to succeed. Whatever the cause of anxiety, the cure was love and trust between two people.

In addition to reading what others had said about knowledge, the seminar itself was an example of how one obtains knowledge. The supportive, anxiety-free environment of our seminar is a simple idea, although it may be difficult to achieve. The idea is not unanimously endorsed by teachers or students; we, however, found it liberating. The students studied with joy and a sense of ownership and personal meaning. Shaughnessy (1977) observed that, paradoxically, we tend to discover what we as individuals have to say by talking with others. Our discussions were not only an aid to memory and an occasion for sharing ideas and insights; they were also for the creation of ideas and insights. Knowledge was created by the process of discussion.

Is this single class too specific and too idiosyncratic to be of general interest? Is the success of a program dependent only on the personalities of the participants? Ideas seem to remain recognizable as they diffuse through our culture even though they are expressed by and influenced by different personalities. The Impressionist painters are associated with a common idea even though each is different. George Balanchine and Jerome Robbins found inspiration in Fred Astaire, but each responded in a personal way. Historically, ideas can be traced in art, dance, social science, mathematics, and so on. The same applies to teaching and learning. There are new ideas to be discovered and shared. Although local adaptations may differ, similarities will be evident.

Insights may come from a single experience, but they are supported by a larger framework of experiences and reading. Polanyi (1964, p. 163) describes how the scientific enterprise is laced with a network of trust among specialists: "Indeed, nobody knows more than a tiny fragment of science well enough to judge its validity and value at first hand. For the rest he has to rely on views accepted at second hand on the authority of a community of people accredited as scientists. . . . Each recognizes as scientists a number of others by whom he is recognized as such in return, and these relations form chains which transmit these mutual recognitions at second hand through the whole community."

The participants of the seminar came together from several disciplines. How can we apply the lessons learned to those disciplines? A goal for me is to find ways of bringing the same joy, the same personal ownership, and the same kind of sharing and creation of knowledge that we experienced to the teaching of mathematics. Some might argue that such a goal is impossible to achieve because a subject like mathematics deals with facts — hard, stubborn facts.

The perception of facts, however, is not without ambiguities. A fact is recognized within a context of theory, and may be invisible in another context. Even a collection of facts has many possible meanings. The recognition of facts and their association with meaning are human activities. Human imagination is a primary requirement. Neither the discipline nor its facts stands alone without imagination.

Mathematics, even though it is abstract, is knowledge to be obtained, and the method by which it is obtained is not exceptional. When mathematicians talk with each other, they talk not as logical machines, but as persons. Their communication can be easy and fertile because they share each other's values as mathematicians.

My timidity, and my fear of being considered sentimental, came from my own encounters with undergraduate and graduate education as a student and as a teacher. I do not think that my encounters were so unusual, because the unanimous feeling of the students was that the love and trust that pervaded our seminar made that seminar a rare experience. Kauffman (1968, p. 13) states: "Though scholarly research has taught us much about the environment and developmental circumstances of learning and growth, we largely ignore this knowledge, even in teaching those disciplines which have told us most about the process of human development." The environment and conditions of our usual education are transparent to us, like the air we breathe. An exceptional situation helps us to notice what we had previously taken for granted.

Some authors, whom I have subsequently discovered, were not timid. Erikson, I have already mentioned. Burtt (1967, pp. 243–245) remarks, "In its true meaning, love is then just what we have described as free and open responsiveness. . . . The objectivity sought by the scientist reveals his insistence that any acceptable result of his work must be capable of verification by other competent inquirers; and without sensitivity to the experience of others and to the standards generally approved in his field, how could such a new result be intelligently sought? Another example is agreement between investigators, which became more and more influential in the course of history as a criterion of truth. . . . Telling the truth . . . is one of the ways in which love is expressed; and we well know that when love is absent words can and will deceive."

The committee on the Student in Higher Education observes: "To teach the subject matter and ignore the realities of the student's life and the social systems of the college is hopelessly naive. . . . The chief goal of the college and university is to train and develop the human intellect, extending the power of independent and balanced thought and deepening the powers of discrimination and critical expression. But it is no longer possible to take a narrow view of intelligence as academic knowledge, isolating cognitive growth from moral growth and the general maturation of the person" (Kauffman, 1968, p. 8). It is not obvious how to translate these ideas to college teaching, although the remarks are addressed to college teachers and administrators.

The committee rejects the "body of knowledge" tradition of curriculum building and asserts that the proliferation of facts, fields, and modes of knowing makes "coverage of the body" a vain hope. I would go further and say that a narrow focus on the body of knowledge of a discipline is counterproductive. A narrow focus actually diminishes comprehension of specialized content. Specialized knowledge cannot be obtained in isolation from its supporting surroundings, or in isolation from the personal feelings of the learners and teachers.

Burtt (1967, p. 246) supports this notion: "The principles which have emerged as essential to true knowledge of persons are essential to true knowledge of everything . . . for love is the only true source of knowledge and without it we lose our ability to learn and to understand. . . . For love, in its widest meaning, is simply an intense, positive interest in an object. . . . The intrinsic bond between love and the quest for truth holds then with no qualification."

The seminar centered around questions of how we obtain knowledge. It was the process of our quest and our reflection on that process that turned unexpected insights into general principles. Those insights transcended the disciplines that were represented, and taught us things about all levels of education that we had not previously noticed.

Now my surprise is not about a student's insightful answer; but whereas I thought a new frontier had been discovered, I now see that it is a well-marked path! Why was that path so obscure to me? Have the years of concentration on specialized or technical knowledge distracted me from real knowledge?

A well-known mathematician writes about a related incident. He describes his experience teaching an elementary course about the New Math. "The assigned text was personally embarrassing. Its preface was replete with reference to committee guidelines, some of which I had written myself during my term as chairman of the committee. Surely this dry and pedantic book, with tedious applications of the associative law, was not what we had envisioned as the outcome of those recommendations! Where was the sense of reality, the ties with the schoolroom, the special insights into the difficulty children have with understanding mathematical concepts? I reread the committee outlines and found that these other aspects were mentioned, but smothered beneath the weight of algebraic structure" (Buck, 1973, p. 2).

What is it that victimizes the author, teacher, and students? What motivates an author to jettison the heart and spirit of the committee's recommendations and to present the technical residue as if it were the whole story? What standard is served by the department in choosing that book as the assigned text? What is lost by the teacher and students if they limit the scope of the course to the text? These questions do not refer only to mathematics courses. "Many educators feel that whereas a physical science course gives technical knowledge, a humanities course provides other knowledge. This is not so. With the current organization of teaching, nearly all university classes are geared to teach only technical knowledge. The exceptions are due not to the substance or arrangement of the curricula . . . but to the genius of the individual professors" (Siu, 1957, p. 92).

We are all victimized by a self-imposed limitation on the aims of education in general and the goals of specific courses in particular. Although every discipline would be described as more than just a collection of facts to be memorized or techniques to be mastered, generations of teachers and students have given their major, and sometimes, exclusive attention to only the facts and techniques. The environments of learning and the processes of learning have been taken for granted as the medium, while we attended, we thought, to the message.

References

Buck, R. C. "Two Experiments in Teaching." *Mathematics News*. Boston: Houghton Mifflin, March 1973.

Burtt, E. A. *In Search of Philosophic Understanding*. New York: New American Library, 1967.

Erikson, E. H. *Insight and Responsibility*. New York: Norton, 1964.

Kauffman, J. F. *The Student in Higher Education*. New Haven, Conn.: The Hazen Foundation, 1968.

Polanyi, M. *Personal Knowledge*. New York: Harper & Row, 1964.

Shaughnessy, M. *Errors and Expectations*. New York: Oxford University Press, 1977.

Siu, R. G. H. *The Tao of Science*. Cambridge, Mass.: M.I.T. Press, 1957.

Tobias, S. *Overcoming Math Anxiety*. New York: Norton, 1978.

Alvin M. White is professor of mathematics at Harvey Mudd College of the Claremont Consortium. From 1977 to 1981 he was the initiator-director of the project New Interdisciplinary, Holistic Approaches to Teaching and Learning that was supported by the Fund for the Improvement of Postsecondary Education. The project, which started as informal discussions with a growing group of colleagues, had among its goals the integration of science and humanities in regular classes.

Personal observations on the natural history of some interdisciplinary programs are presented with reference to sources about others.

Reflections on the Past; Hopes for the Future

Alvin M. White

How does an interdisciplinary program get started? Is every instance of inter-disciplinarity a program? What sources of ideas and references are available?

There are many approaches to interdisciplinarity, but there are some common characteristics about programs that have survived for a few years. An important, perhaps essential, feature is an individual or group who is interested in sustaining such a program. Even casual, spontaneous conversations must occur in a nurturing or at least nonhostile environment that includes the time as well as the place. A sustained series of conversations that evolve into substantial discussions, and perhaps lead to an educational program, will rarely happen without some leadership and guidance. Such leadership is especially noticeable after the individual or group departs, and the apparently self-sustaining discussions or program simply end.

The project, New Interdisciplinary, Holistic Approaches to Teaching and Learning, began in Claremont from meaningful conversations about science and its contexts. Conversations between two persons became discussions among seven, and, eventually, discussions among thirty about the structure of scientific revolutions in geology, science and human values, non-Darwinian evolution, subjectivity and objectivity in science, and other topics. These discussions continued on a regular biweekly basis for about a year. When I went on sabbatical leave, the discussions stopped; then resumed when I returned. If

A. White (Ed.). *New Directions for Teaching and Learning: Interdisciplinary Teaching*, no. 8. San Francisco: Jossey-Bass, December 1981

an activity is to be independent of a particular person or group, then an organizational structure must be created.

The discussions convinced us that our formal teaching should honestly reflect the interdisciplinary structure of knowledge that we were discovering informally. None of us, however, felt broadly enough educated or bold enough to attempt a radical reorganization of our teaching. We applied to the Fund for the Improvement of Postsecondary Education to support our mutual education. The first proposal was unsuccessful. One reviewer wrote that it was "trivial"; another declared it "impossible!" We received a grant on the second application.

The project, which began as the personal vision of a few, became a major part of faculty culture. Approaches that were viewed with skepticism became accepted and expected. Ideas, which were on the radical fringes of academe, about integrating the sciences and the humanities moved into the mainstream of desired educational outcomes. Some faculty members who were timid about trying new modes of teaching, or introducing new content such as values and ethics, were supported and encouraged by the newly created setting.

Although we did not advertise our interdisciplinary seminars, more and more colleagues asked to participate. Our mailing list of participants soon reached 200 and, during the second and third year, announcements and newsletters were sent to almost 1,000 participants. Questions and comments stimulated many faculty members to view their own subjects in new ways and to find new colleagues with whom to collaborate or argue. As they left the early meetings, philosophers asked physicists about the latest interpretation of quantum mechanics so they could adapt their philosophy. Physicists, in turn, asked philosophers how to understand Aristotle, or the meaning of a statement by Descartes, or by Newton.

Questions of content led to questions of form. As our concept of knowledge broadened, many of us became concerned with the processes of teaching and learning. We had discussions and workshops on teaching beginning writing, then on "writing across the disciplines." Other workshops were concerned with learning and teaching styles, and with the developmental ideas of Piaget and William Perry. A workshop on improving classroom teaching skills was particularly successful and well received. Other colleges and groups, including the R.O.T.C., arranged to duplicate the workshop at other locations. The workshop dealt with teaching and learning problems such as setting a learning climate, how to encourage participation and interaction, developing questioning strategies, leading discussions, and so on. Many participants reported making immediate use of their new skills and insights.

The success of the project illustrates the power of ideas — more, it illustrates the power of *shared* ideas. The seminar announcements and other mailings contained one, two, or three pages of substantial explanation, summary, or other information about the subject. Although everyone who received a seminar announcement did not attend, almost everyone read it. Many, including those who had no other contact except the mailed announcements, remarked that the project was one of the most exciting things they remembered.

The success of the project also illustrates that faculty members, as well as others, are eager to share ideas and participate in mind-stretching activities. Some colleagues remarked that this project fulfilled a "yearning" of theirs. Formal and informal interdisciplinary discussions among faculty members are, in a sense, the quintessence of academic culture.

Norbert Weiner, in the introduction to his book *Cybernetics*, mentions the monthly series of discussions organized by Dr. Arturo Rosenblueth at the Harvard Medical School. In the foreword to *Space Structures* by Arthur L. Loeb, Cyril Stanley Smith refers to the origin of some of the ideas in the discussions of the Philomorphs — a group including biologists, mathematicians, metallurgists, artists, architects, sociologists, and others who met because of their common interests in underlying patterns. In several memoirs about Leo Szilard at the University of Chicago, the weekly wide-ranging discussions involving colleagues from diverse disciplines are remembered fondly.

There are informal lunchtime or evening discussions on many campuses. These are often sources of new insights, new courses and programs, and much personal satisfaction. Each of them of which I am aware is organized and sustained by one or two individuals.

Why do such exercises of human spirit and intellect flourish on some campuses? Is it an accident that certain individuals are present or that certain groups of people happen to meet and establish a relationship? Can a setting be created that would encourage such relationships? Is there a special mood that can be recognized or sensed in those places where there is an intellectual vitality?

These questions are close to the problem that Plato raised in the *Meno*. "If you really know nothing of the nature of virtue," Meno asks Socrates, "how do you propose to find out? How can we ask for something if we do not know what that something is?"

Without taking on the larger questions raised by Plato, I suggest that a campus is influenced by the values and world views of the campus leaders, including the administration. If intellectual vitality is valued then that viewpoint will be communicated.

On a personal note, I was not aware of the interdisciplinary interests of many of my colleagues until I asked some of them and was referred to more by others. After becoming the director of an interdisciplinary project, I found many new colleagues who shared my interdisciplinary interests. It is possible, when following a normal routine, to restrict one's contact within a narrow range of ideas and disciplines. There may be many potential colleagues who would respond enthusiastically to a chance to cross disciplinary boundaries. The range and scope of my own circle of colleagues and ideas have been tremendously enlarged and enriched since I became a project director.

The report by Robert Belknap and Richard Kuhns, *Tradition and Innovation* (Columbia University Press, 1977), describes the discussions and seminars on general education at Columbia University. The publication of the book and seminar reports was supported by the Rockefeller Foundation and the Carnegie Corporation because the value of these discussions reached far beyond Columbia.

Descriptions of many courses and programs can be found in the annual reports of the Fund for the Improvement of Postsecondary Education, *Resources for Change.* There have been over 800 projects.

The six *Reports on Teaching* published by *Change Magazine* describe innovative ideas. The *Yellow Pages of Undergraduate Innovation* published by Change Magazine Press is another source of programs and ideas. The *EVIST Resource Directory* available from the Office of Science Education, American Association for the Advancement of Science, 1776 Massachusetts Ave., N.W., Washington, D.C., 20036, describes hundreds of courses and programs in science, technology, human values, ethics, philosophical perspectives, and much more.

Some other books and articles that have stimulated interdisciplinary activities and interests are discussed here.

Kockelmans, J. J. (Ed.), *Interdisciplinarity and Higher Education,* The Pennsylvania State University Press, University Park, 1979, is an anthology which illustrates the range of interdisciplinarity. A selective list of programs and a bibliography are included.

"Idea tasting is the intellectual analog of wine tasting. It is a process in which ideas are held up to the clear light of reason for analysis, wafted toward the mind to catch the scent of their intellectual bouquet, and caught lightly on the mind's edge to savor their substance and flavor before being ingested." These poetic words come from Sister Eileen Rice, O.P., the author of *Idea Tasting,* which is a book of readings and suggestions for her course. The book is available for about $10 from the author at Siena Heights College, 1247 East Siena Heights Drive, Adrian, Michigan 49221.

If you are not aware of the *Dictionary of the History of Ideas,* edited by Philip P. Weiner, and published by Charles Scribner's Sons, 1973, then I strongly recommend becoming acquainted with this heroic five volume collection of selected pivotal ideas. Your library should have it in the reference section. Personal paperback editions are available for about $100.

Marjorie Hope Nicolson has written two books which relate the sciences and literature of the seventeenth and eighteenth centuries: *The Breaking of the Circle — Studies in the Effect of the "New Science" on Seventeenth Century Poetry,* Columbia University Press, New York, 1962, and *Newton Demands the Muse — Newton's Opticks and the Eighteenth Century Poets,* Princeton University Press, Princeton, 1966, set a high standard for such studies. Henry Margenau is professor emeritus of physics and natural philosophy at Yale and one of the founders of the Center for Integrative Education. The Center, whose aim is to provide methods and materials to overcome the divisiveness of modern education, publishes the journal *Main Currents of Modern Thought.* Margenau's 1950 book, *The Nature of Physical Reality,* which inspired a generation of scholars, has been reprinted by Ox Box Press, Woodbridge, Connecticut.

Integrative Principles of Modern Thought is an anthology that grew out of the experience of the Center for Integrative Education. The editor is Henry Margenau and the publisher is Gordon and Breach, New York, 1972.

Philipp Frank was professor of physics at Harvard where he supplied the missing link — the philosophy of science to bridge the chasm between science and humanities. His book *Philosophy of Science*, Prentice-Hall, Englewood Cliffs, N.J., 1957, traces the history of science from Aristotle to Einstein illustrating how philosophy has always been a part of scientific progress.

More recent books which analyze the process of science are Gerald Holton's *Thematic Origins of Scientific Thought — Kepler to Einstein*, Harvard University Press, Cambridge, Mass., 1973; *The Scientific Imagination: Case Studies*, Cambridge University Press, 1978; and Stephen Toulmin's *Human Understanding*, Princeton University Press, 1972.

The project, "New Interdisciplinary, Holistic Approaches to Teaching and Learning" had as part of its ethos the encouragement and support of innovation. We not only welcomed new models of teaching and new content in traditional courses, but also new ways of understanding and seeing. For some people certain ideas are well established, while for other people those same ideas are still controversial or below the threshold of their awareness.

The article by Eugene S. Ferguson, "The Mind's Eye: Nonverbal Thought in Technology," *Science*, 1977, *197*, 827–836, made an important contribution to our knowledge. The author shows how thinking with pictures is an essential strand of technological development and design. He also describes some catastrophes that resulted from designs that neglected visualization. The article elicited over 200 letters of strong support from many readers including physicians and musicians.

Rudolf Arnheim has been writing books and articles on visual thinking for many years. His book *Visual Thinking*, University of California Press, Berkeley, 1969, discusses the thinking process that accompanies seeing.

Visual thinking in engineering education at Stanford is described in the book by Robert H. McKim, *Experiences in Visual Thinking*, Brooks/Cole, Monterey, Calif., 1972.

Books that consider the visual sense in another context are C. H. Waddington's *Behind Appearance* (a study of the relations between painting and the natural sciences in this century), The M.I.T. Press, 1970, and E. H. Gombrich's *Art and Illusion — A Study in the Psychology of Pictorial Representation*, Princeton University Press, 1969.

Norwood Russell Hanson was a pioneer in the philosophy of science. His book *Patterns of Discovery — An Inquiry into the Conceptual Foundations of Science*, Cambridge University Press, 1972, considers the perception of facts through our visual sense.

The psychologist Robert E. Ornstein extends the consideration of how we perceive things in two books: *The Nature of Human Consciousness: A Book of Readings*, W. H. Freeman, San Francisco, 1973, and *The Psychology of Consciousness*, W. H. Freeman, San Francisco, 1972.

A major thesis of the 1973 book "is that two major modes of consciousness exist in man, the intellectual and its complement, the intuitive. Contemporary science (and, indeed, much of western culture) has predominantly emphasized the intellectual mode and has filtered out rich sources of evidence: meditation, 'mysticism,' non-ordinary reality, the influence of 'the body' on 'the mind.' In part, this book is intended to open inquiry into that inelegant, tacit, 'other' side of ourselves."

The discovery of the tacit "other" side of ourselves reminds one of the discovery of the developmental theories of Piaget and of William Perry's *Forms of Intellectual and Ethical Development in the College Years*, Holt, Rinehart and Winston, New York, 1970.

In the area of consciousness, mention should be made of two books by Marilyn Ferguson: *The Brain Revolution* (1973) and *The Aquarian Conspiracy* (1980) published by J. P. Tarcher, Inc., Los Angeles. Marilyn Ferguson also publishes two newsletters: *Leading Edge Bulletin* and *Brain Mind Bulletin*, which are available from P.O. Box 42247 and P.O. Box 42211, Los Angeles, Calif. 90042.

The *Brain Mind Bulletin* made me aware of the special issue of the *Journal of Humanistic Psychology* (Vol. 21, No. 2, Spring 1981) that was devoted to Johnston College and Humanistic Higher Education. Articles about the beginnings and endings of Johnston College at the University of Redlands and similar efforts at the Experimental College at San Francisco State College and Kresge College at University of California, Santa Cruz are presented. Single copies are available for $4.00 from J.H.P. Circulation Office, 325 Ninth Street, San Francisco, Calif. 94103.

In order to end on a note of hope, I'll mention "a view of what education might become" as explained by Carl R. Rogers' *Freedom to Learn*, Charles E. Merrill, Columbus, 1969. The issue of *Education* (Vol. 95, No. 2, Winter 1974) is devoted to articles about experiences of teachers who were inspired to teach their classes guided by *Freedom to Learn*. The levels and disciplines were varied. A related article about a course in thermodynamics is described in J. G. Mullen, *American Journal of Physics* (Vol. 43, No. 4, April 1975, pp. 354–360).

This listing is neither exhaustive nor extensive. It is a personal survey of material that I have found useful. Its extent has been limited by space.

Alvin M. White is professor of Mathematics at Harvey Mudd College of the Claremont Consortium. From 1977 to 1981 he was the initiator-director of the project New Interdisciplinary, Holistic Approaches to Teaching and Learning that was supported by the Fund for the Improvement of Postsecondary Education. The project, which started as informal discussions with a growing group of colleagues, had among its goals the integration of science and humanities in regular classes.

Index